D1561949

We Will Always Be Here

A Guide to Exploring
and Understanding the
History of LGBTQ+
Activism in Wisconsin

Jenny Kalvaitis

Kristen Whitson

WISCONSIN HISTORICAL SOCIETY PRESS

JUL - 2021

Published by the Wisconsin Historical Society Press
Publishers since 1855

The Wisconsin Historical Society helps people connect to the past by collecting,
preserving, and sharing stories. Founded in 1846, the Society is one of the nation's finest
historical institutions.
Join the Wisconsin Historical Society: wisconsinhistory.org/membership

© 2021 by the State Historical Society of Wisconsin

For permission to reuse material from *We Will Always Be Here: A Guide to Exploring and
Understanding the History of LGBTQ+ Activism in Wisconsin* (ISBN 978-0-87020-961-1;
e-book ISBN 978-0-87020-962-8), please access www.copyright.com or contact the
Copyright Clearance Center, Inc. (CCC), 222 Rosewood Drive, Danvers, MA 01923,
978-750-8400. CCC is a not-for-profit organization that provides licenses and registration
for a variety of users.

Front cover images, clockwise from top left: Tammy Baldwin, Dick Wagner, and Kathleen
Nichols in 1987, courtesy of Dick Wagner; Edgar Hellum in 1935, Mineral Point Library
Archives; Donna Coleman ca. 1965, courtesy of the University of Wisconsin–Madison
Archives; members of Bi?Shy?Why? in 1993, courtesy of the University of Wisconsin–
Madison Archives; Ted Pierce ca. 1924, WHI IMAGE ID 71483; and Lou Sullivan in 1966,
courtesy of Gay, Lesbian, Bisexual, Transgender Historical Society.

Back cover images, clockwise from top left: Bob Neal ca. 1940, Mineral Point Library
Archives; Judy Greenspan ca. 1973, WHI IMAGE ID 59050; and Meika Alberici in 1978,
WHI IMAGE ID 67962.

Printed in the United States of America
Cover design by Andrew Brozyna
Text design and typesetting by Mayfly Design

25 24 23 22 21   1 2 3 4 5

Library of Congress Cataloging-in-Publication Data
Names: Kalvaitis, Jenny, author. | Whitson, Kristen, author.
Title: We will always be here : a guide to exploring and understanding the
  history of LGBTQ+ activism in Wisconsin / Jenny Kalvaitis and Kristen
  Whitson.
Description: [Madison] : Wisconsin Historical Society Press, [2021] |
  Includes bibliographical references and index.
Identifiers: LCCN 2020047573 (print) | LCCN 2020047574 (ebook) | ISBN
  9780870209611 (paperback) | ISBN 9780870209628 (ebook)
Subjects: LCSH: Sexual minorities—Wisconsin—History—Juvenile literature.
  | Gay liberation movement—Wisconsin—History—Juvenile literature.
Classification: LCC HQ73.3.U62 W653 2021 (print) | LCC HQ73.3.U62 (ebook)
  | DDC 306.7609775—dc23
LC record available at https://lccn.loc.gov/2020047573
LC ebook record available at https://lccn.loc.gov/2020047574

♾ The paper used in this publication meets the minimum requirements of the American
National Standard for Information Sciences—Permanence of Paper for Printed Library
Materials, ANSI Z39.48-19

*For Jodie Jens, Judy Reynolds, all the brave LGBTQ+
folks who have helped make the world a better place,
and all the young people who are inspired to do the same.*

Publication of this book was made possible in part through generous gifts from:

Mr. Charles Bauer and Mr. Charles Beckwith

David Bedri and Jon Sorenson

Sue Riseling and Joanne Berg

Paula Bonner and Ann Schaffer

Frances Breit and Julie D'Acci

Gary Brown and Paul Hayes

Barbara Constans and Deb Rohde

Paul Gibler and Thomas DeChant

Bob Dowd and Marge Schmidt

Julie Eckenwalder and Constance Anderson

William and Lynne Eich

Renee Herber and Tamara Packard

Joanne Holland and Margie Rosenberg

Kim Karcher

Scott and Mary Kolar

Donald Lamb

Phil Levy

Hank Lufler and Mike Gerdes

Katharine Lyall

Scott and Megin McDonell

Eileen Mershart and Sarah Hole

Mike and Sally Miley

Anne Monks

Richard Petran

Purple Moon Foundation, Inc. – Dale Leibowitz

Timothy Radelet

Mary Lou Roberts

Susan Schaffer and Joan Hinckley

Robert Stipicevich and Scott Short

Mary Strickland and Marie Barroquillo

Howard Sweet

Mike Verveer

William Wartmann

Mark Webster and Ryan Brown

Susan Zaeske

Jaime Zimmerman

Contents

Introduction

The past is full of stories just waiting to be uncovered. Lesbian, gay, bisexual, transgender, queer, and other members of the LGBTQ+ community have been present throughout human history, even though they appear in few textbooks. Looking back through Wisconsin's history, LGBTQ+ folks can be found in literature and the arts, on the battlefield and in political office, in restaurants and on farms, in the public eye and in everyday life. For example:

- Lorraine Hansberry, a lesbian and author of the play *A Raisin in the Sun*, attended the University of Wisconsin–Madison in the late 1940s. She won the New York Drama Critics' Circle Award in 1959. Not only was she the youngest playwright to receive the honor, she was also the first African American and the fifth woman to do so.

- Barry Lynn was a gay man and professional dancer who choreographed more than five hundred dances in his career. In 1978, he founded a center for expressive dance in Ladysmith, Wisconsin, with his partner, Michael Doran.

- Robert Peters of Eagle River, Wisconsin, fought in Germany during World War II (1939–1945). He served as an infantryman, clerk typist, and chaplain's assistant while climbing to the rank of sergeant. He wrote the memoir *For You, Lili Marlene: A Memoir of World War II*. In it, he recalled having to suppress his identity, occasionally being called out, and fantasizing about other men.[1]

- Lorena Hickok from East Troy, Wisconsin, was a well-known and respected journalist for the Associated Press starting in the 1920s. In 1928, she was assigned to interview Eleanor Roosevelt during her husband's presidential campaign. Hickok and Roosevelt developed a romantic relationship that spanned decades.[2]

However they refer to themselves—as gay, lesbian, bi, trans, queer, nonbinary, gender nonconforming, questioning, or by some other adjective—LGBTQ+ people are simply people. They work in every imaginable field, and they live in every city and town on the map. This book is full of ordinary, extraordinary people living their lives and working for change in Wisconsin.

And yet LGBTQ+ history is full of stories that are rarely featured in schools, museums, or popular publications. Why is this? The stories of some LGBTQ+ individuals have been suppressed due to prejudice. In some cases, the people who fund textbooks, curate museum ex-

The more I learn of history, the more I realize what I've missed!

hibits, and write articles have wished to create a mainstream history rather than include a wide diversity of human experience. In other cases, people have been justifiably afraid to share their own stories. For many years (and even today), lots of LGBTQ+ people have kept their true identities hidden. They have rightly feared negative outcomes that could result from being open about their sex, gender, or sexuality.

The playwright Lorraine Hansberry attended the University of Wisconsin–Madison from 1948 to 1950. She is standing in front of UW's Agricultural Hall in this 1948 photo. She was not out for decades but identified as a lesbian in her private writings toward the end of her life. PHOTO USE COURTESY OF THE LORRAINE HANSBERRY LITERARY TRUST, LHLT.ORG

It is time to look back and begin learning these stories. It is time to take them off the shelf and out of the closet. It is time to put them in the hands of people like you, who can use the past to build a better future. The time has come for an inclusive, accurate history. The next generation should not have to fight the same battles that we have been fighting for decades.

Framework

This book is about the actions that LGBTQ+ people took throughout Wisconsin's history to live their best lives and change our world for the better. In each chapter, you'll find different examples of historical activism. Some may look familiar to you, while some may challenge your assumptions about what activism can be. First, you will learn some basic details about the people involved in these actions. Next, you will explore primary sources that are the records (and, in some cases, the tools) of that activism—diary entries, newspaper articles, posters, love letters, photographs, and more. These sources transcend time. No matter how long ago they were created, they can be relevant to you today. We hope that after exploring them, you will realize you have the power to create a record of your own history.

Many stories have been lost to history because there is no proper record and no person to remember the events. Because the stories of LGBTQ+ folks (sometimes spelled folx) are so rarely shared, we often lose the chance to learn from their experiences. Sometimes, people begin fighting for a cause without realizing that the cause has had supporters for decades or generations. It is up to us to explore and learn from the past so that we can make informed decisions in the present and bring about change in the future.

This book is not a comprehensive history of every LGBTQ+ story, action, or movement in Wisconsin. It is only a starting point.

In order to choose the sources for this book, we turned to teens. Through an online survey, we presented teens across Wisconsin with dozens of primary sources and asked what spoke to them. The feedback they provided helped us shape the book. You will find their

> I was surprised to see many of these pieces that have to do directly with Wisconsin history because I had never heard these people's stories before.

insights and opinions sprinkled throughout these pages, appearing in comment bubbles like the one above. As you read, we encourage you to closely consider the documents, look at additional sources (see page 124 for our Additional Resources list), and explore these topics further.

This book is not necessarily meant to be read from cover to cover. Rather, read it in the way that feels right to you. We hope it provides examples of historical activism that inspire you no matter who you are or how you identify. There is no one definition of an activist. You can follow the paths of the many people who came before you, or you can forge your own path.

No matter who you are, we hope you find something in this book that speaks to you. Are you out and proud? Great! We hope you gather inspiration and a sense of solidarity from those who came before you. Are you unsure of who you are at this moment in time? You are not alone! We hope you begin to see glimpses of yourself in this history and gain a new understanding of your identity. Are you an ally wondering how to support your LGBTQ+ friends? Your help is needed! We hope you expand your understanding of this history and learn about ways you can contribute. Are you just beginning your education about LGBTQ+ issues? We hope you reflect on this history and think critically about what it all means. Whoever you are, wherever you live, and whatever your life experience, there are always more stories to be heard, and there's always more learning to be done.

Barry Lynn's style of modern dance involved the generous use of fabrics. He is pictured here in 1999 on the grounds of the center for dance he founded with his partner in Ladysmith, Wisconsin. PHOTO BY J. SHIMON & J. LINDEMANN

Analyzing Primary Sources

As we mentioned earlier, this book features primary sources introduced by brief paragraphs written by your authors to add context. The primary sources are firsthand accounts of topics by people who had direct connections to those topics. Primary sources can be letters, photographs, diary entries, or other items that were created or present as the history was being made. While some of the primary sources in this book contain misspellings and grammatical errors, we have chosen to present the sources exactly as they originally appeared. Our introductions to each primary source are secondary sources—information written about the primary sources to interpret or add details to the story.

By introducing the primary sources with a bit of context, we hope to weave together a story of social and emotional learning, activist history, and identity.

- Social and emotional learning is the process of developing self-awareness and social awareness. It's how we learn to make responsible decisions, manage relationships, and understand our own emotions. Every story in this book includes examples of social and emotional learning.

- Activist history describes the history of people who have taken actions against the status quo. As we mentioned earlier, activism can take many forms. It doesn't have to be public or loud, like marching or running for office. It can be personal or quiet, like writing a letter or joining a club, just as long as it is being done to change society.

- Identity is complex. It would be impossible for us to fully describe and do justice to the identity of each individual featured in this book. We have done our best to give you a glimpse into their many different qualities, personalities, and beliefs.

Primary sources are important in part because they allow us to look at past actions and events through a new lens. For instance, many people living in Mineral Point in the 1930s may have assumed that Bob Neal and Edgar Hellum were just

> *I thought history was all "LGBTQ+ Bad!" and nothing good happened until recently.*

business partners. But the letters that Edgar and Bob exchanged (see page 59 for one of these letters) allow us to understand that they were romantic partners, too. Primary sources like these prove that LGBTQ+ people have been present in and made significant contributions to their communities throughout history.

As you read this book, we encourage you to use the Library of Congress's framework for analyzing primary sources: observe, reflect, and question.

- While observing, you might ask yourself: "What do you notice first? What do you notice that you didn't expect? What do you notice that you can't explain?"

- You can reflect on the sources by considering these questions: "Where do you think this came from? Why do you think somebody made this? What do you think was happening when this was made? Who do you think was the audience for this item? Why do you think this item is important?"

- Finally, ask your own questions: "What do you wonder about who/what/when/where/why/how?"[3]

You could also look at the book *Thinking Like a Historian* by Nikki Mandell and Bobbie Malone. The book asks us to consider the causes and effects of past events. What has changed and what has remained the same? What do you know about how people in the past viewed their world and how past decisions or actions affected future choices? How do you think the past helps us make sense of the present?[4]

No matter what tools you use, you will get the most out of this book by thinking critically about each source. A thoughtful and curious person never finds all the answers. Their work is never truly done, because they are always asking questions and always learning.

Vocabulary and Pronouns

While reading this book, you may come across terms that are new to you or terms that have had different meanings over time. We encourage you to make a note of those words and phrases and to look up their definitions to expand your understanding. We've included some resources for vocabulary definitions

Robert Peters from Eagle River, Wisconsin, was a solider in World War II, and he wrote about his sexual orientation in his memoirs. REPRINTED BY PERMISSION OF THE UNIVERSITY OF WISCONSIN PRESS. © 1995 BY THE BOARD OF REGENTS OF THE UNIVERSITY OF WISCONSIN SYSTEM. ALL RIGHTS RESERVED.

in the Additional Resources section at the end of this book.

Words, phrases, titles, and terms change all the time—that's the nature of language. As a result, some of the primary sources in this book contain outdated terms. For example, a couple sources use the word *transsexual* to refer to people we would describe today as *transgender*. In other sources, the word *homosexual* refers to people who might prefer the words *gay man* or *lesbian* today. In these examples and others, terms that were once considered appropriate may strike us as old-fashioned and possibly even offensive. Still, it is important to present these words as they originally appeared in the primary sources because it gives us the opportunity to consider how and why language has changed.

We chose to use the acronym LGBTQ+ throughout this book because at the time of this book's publication, it is commonly used to describe the lesbian, gay, bisexual, transgender, and queer community. We feel the + makes an attempt at the inclusivity that a longer acronym with additional letters might convey.

When describing transgender people, we use the pronouns the

Lorena Hickok, from East Troy, Wisconsin, was one of Eleanor Roosevelt's romantic partners. The two met while Hickok was covering President Franklin Roosevelt and his family for the Associated Press. She is pictured here in 1926.
HENNEPIN COUNTY LIBRARY

individuals chose for themselves whenever possible. We don't always know what pronouns some historical figures would have chosen for themselves, but we can make educated guesses based on their demonstrated desires to be known as men, women, or nonbinary individuals. We have also tried to avoid using deadnames, the names that transgender people were assigned at birth and no longer use after they've transitioned.[5] Although the primary sources associated with these people sometimes contain incorrect pronouns or deadnames, we have not altered any text in the primary sources. We feel it is important for you to see the sources exactly as they appeared and to consider the implications of the language they contain.

Historical Perspectives

Pre-Stonewall

LGBTQ+ history goes back thousands of years. As the title of R. Richard Wagner's book about Wisconsin's early gay history declares, we've been here all along.[6] For as long as there have been people in Wisconsin, there have been people who we would celebrate as LGBTQ+ today, though that acronym is a modern invention. Before the 1800s, written documents refer to people taking part in same-sex behavior, but they do not refer to individuals *as* homosexuals. The understanding of homosexuality as a part of one's identity occurred after people began using the word *homosexual* in the late 1800s as a label for people who participated in same-sex activities.

A 1953 study of Ho-Chunk sexuality revealed to mainstream society that the Ho-Chunk have honored and accepted their people who are now known as two-spirit for hundreds of years. Males who are two-spirit take on certain female roles in their communities.[7] In fact, two-spirit people have now been commonly acknowledged in many Native cultures, not just those in Wisconsin. When Europeans in North America encountered the Ho-Chunk in the early 1600s, they applied the term *berdache* to the two-spirit Ho-Chunk people. However, *berdache*, originally derived from the Persian word for a male sexual slave or boy prostitute, did not accurately describe two-spirit people, who "blended gender roles" by dressing in women's clothing and sometimes marrying other men.[8] Some Ho-Chunk people, and many other indigenous people, identify as two-spirit to this day.

Throughout most of American history, evidence of homosexuality could be most easily found in court cases. Until relatively recently, the law defined homosexual acts as behaviors that must be stopped and prevented. Court cases reveal that LGBTQ+ people were arrested, publicly mocked, and treated like criminals for taking part in same-sex activities. In some instances, they received such treatment for simply appearing to be nonbinary or gender nonconforming. Cross-dressing people were subjected to examinations by medical or court-appointed professionals and had their reproductive parts checked to determine their sex. Thomas(ine) Hall caused a controversy in 1629 in Virginia for wearing clothing that most people considered to be appropriate only for the "opposite sex." As women and men were expected to fulfill quite different roles in colonial America, many people viewed this cross-dressing as a great deception and did not accept Hall's gender fluidity. After Hall was inspected by doctors, the court ruled that Hall was both a man and a woman and forced Hall to wear male and female clothing simultaneously.[9] Almost 350 years later, in 1977, police in Houston, Texas, arrested fifty-three people in one year for disguising their sex.[10]

Wisconsin, then, is not unique in its historically poor treatment of members of the LGBTQ+ community. In the late 1940s and 1950s, college students in Wisconsin were put on probation and even expelled for being a part of the LGBTQ+ community. Psychotherapists tried to "cure" these students. If they refused to undergo treatment, they were often forced to withdraw from school. For example, Blanche, a well-known Madison personality, withdrew from a UW–Madison graduate program in music rather than undergo psychotherapy. In his book about Wisconsin's early gay history *We've Been Here All Along*, R. Richard Wagner (see page 42 for more information on Wagner) explained that Blanche changed to a career "in music education, assisting students who came into the record stores on lower State Street by serving them as an extremely knowledgeable sales clerk."[11] Blanche was not alone. For decades, LGBTQ+ students in Wisconsin faced many disadvantages and had no legal protections against discrimination.

In fact, in the not-so-distant past, Wisconsin had laws that specifically targeted gay men and lesbians. The 1940s and 1950s

The 602 Club in Madison, pictured here in the mid-1960s, was one of the rare establishments that welcomed gay patrons in the years before Stonewall. PHOTO BY JOHN RIGGS

are sometimes referred to as the McCarthy era after Wisconsin senator Joseph McCarthy, who attempted to force gay and lesbian government workers from their jobs. He claimed that they were national security risks because their sexual orientation made them targets for blackmail. During these decades, many LGBTQ+ people "retreated to respectability," or tried to pass as mainstream members of a majority heterosexual and cisgender society.[12] Almost no one was openly gay during this time. Most people chose to live their lives undercover rather than risk the potential consequences of being out.

However, in Madison, Wisconsin, some bars were ahead of their time in welcoming gay people. The 602 Club was named for its address at 602 University Avenue in Madison. It wasn't officially or publicly a "gay bar," but in the 1950s and 1960s, gay men regularly occupied the front half of the bar and straight patrons occupied the back half. The bar's owner, Dudley Howe, was a tolerant man. He welcomed all patrons as long as they weren't bothering anyone else. Unfortunately, the 602 Club was a rare case in Wisconsin and throughout the country at that time.

Stonewall

LGBTQ+ history is often divided into two parts, pre-Stonewall and post-Stonewall. The events that we refer to as Stonewall were so momentous that the word now signifies a major shift in the lives of LGBTQ+ folks in America. But it also refers to a place. The Stonewall Inn was a gay club in Greenwich Village in New York City. When the police raided it on June 28, 1969, the people inside decided to fight back. An uprising began, led in part by gay street youth, lesbians, and trans women of color including Sylvia Rivera, Marsha P. Johnson, and Stormé DeLarverie. Six days of protests and violent conflict between LGBTQ+ folks and law enforcement in the area followed.

In the decades before Stonewall, police officers often targeted businesses rumored to be gay bars, which had a reputation as dangerous, unseemly places. Even after the Stonewall uprising, gay bars in Wisconsin continued to have this reputation.[13] A simple gathering of LGBTQ+ people in a bar could be labeled as disorderly by the police and serve as cause for arrest. For decades, the LGBTQ+ community used workarounds, codes, and (as in the case of the Stonewall Inn) connections that allowed them to gather without attracting attention from the authorities. Occasionally bar-goers received information about a planned police raid before it occurred and were able to avoid being caught. However, on June 28, 1969, at the Stonewall Inn, there was no warning, and the patrons' decision to fight back launched a national social justice movement.

This sign from the Stonewall uprising of 1969 was displayed inside the Stonewall Inn in 2016. The bar became an official national monument that year, honoring the location's importance in the history of the United States. WIKIMEDIA COMMONS; RHODODENDRITES/CREATIVE COMMONS

Post-Stonewall

Societal change takes time. In most cases, one protest, one riot, or one single event cannot change a complex and entrenched system of oppression. However, the individuals involved in events like these are often changed—and charged—by the experience. After standing up for their rights, many activists become energized to engage in a longer fight that might last decades or even centuries, striving toward equality.

After that first night of the Stonewall uprising, follow-up marches, gatherings, and political conversations occurred across the country. In New York City in June 1970, a mass gathering of people identifying as part of the LGBTQ+ community came together to demand respect. Today's gay pride parades are direct descendants of that occasion.[14]

In the weeks and months following Stonewall, an organized gay rights movement grew. The Gay Liberation Front in New York was founded in immediate response to Stonewall. Later, other groups of activists around the country would use the same name, though they were not national organizations. In 1971, the Madison Gay Liberation Front held a convention over Thanksgiving that drew groups from around the country.[15]

This call to action from the newly formed Madison Alliance for Homosexual Equality was published in the University of Wisconsin–Madison's *Daily Cardinal* in November 1969, just five months after the Stonewall uprising. DAILY CARDINAL LGBTQ IMAGES, CIRCA 1960–1990, UAC68, UNIVERSITY OF WISCONSIN–MADISON ARCHIVES, MADISON, WISCONSIN

AN OPEN LETTER TO HOMOSEXUALS

Dear Sirs:

An open letter to campus homosexuals: From an unmentionable entity to the cover of Time, the homosexual life has gained unprecedented national prominence. The straight world wears our clothes, reads our books, uses our slang, sees our movies, and swoons over our idols. Yet most of the good people of America view us with disgust and even outright hatred. (But it's really kind of fun to be a danger to society, isn't it?) Nevertheless, for all the harassment, intimidation, and discrimination, things are looking up: riots in New York, pickets in California, and lobbying in the right places are all making it easier to live the good gay life.

For the thinking man, new freedoms mean new responsibilities. The thinking homosexual man now has the responsibility to respond to the call of the times. The times are here and now, and every last one of us—even the screamingest queens in the bar—has a duty to respond. While blacks act, TA's act, welfare mothers act, American Indians act, we namby-pamby sissies sit timidly by, expecting the straight world to go gay.

Listen, Brother: you and I are an oppressed minority. We're security risks, insurance risks, undesirables and general nuisances. And we're not men because we let them feed us all that crap without so much as a whimper. We keep all the whimpers inside and live our lives in fear, simply because we haven't got the balls to act. Here, in Madison, Wisconsin.

Sure, nobody throws rocks at you at your little table in the Rath. But if you can say, with Jean Cocteau, "I don't want to be just tolerated: it offends my love of beauty and of life," then you will think it is time to act. What we need, here and now, is organization. We need awareness of ourselves and our condition. We need to be men.

This week a group tentatively called The Hallowen is forming on campus. It's a mature group for concerned people. Check the Union bulletin boards for information.

After Stonewall, politicians began seriously discussing laws pertaining to the LGBTQ+ community. Wisconsin was the first state in the nation to pass a nondiscrimination law based on sexual orientation in 1982. By 1983, a council on lesbian and gay issues began drafting an unofficial survey of the state's gay community.[16] Wisconsin became known as the Gay Rights State, and the gay community continued to grow and flourish. As homosexuality was no longer punishable by law in Wisconsin, the state increasingly contributed LGBTQ+ radio and television programs to the national scene. People held picnics, parades, and protests. Schools, streets, and society became safer for LGBTQ+ people. But things were not easy, nor were they perfect. Gay marriage was legalized in various states starting in 2008 and then, ultimately, across the country through federal action in 2015.

Despite the advances and improvements made in recent decades, there is still work to be done in terms of equity, safety, and respect. That is why your involvement is needed in the LGBTQ+ movement today!

Overview

Chapter 1 is about the importance of taking your education into your own hands. By reading about people and issues in the LGBTQ+ community, we not only learn about ourselves and others, but we also form opinions and develop our own beliefs.

Chapter 2 encourages you to write your own story so that the next generation has a new canon of LGBTQ+ literature. Since the Stonewall uprising, a growing number of publications by and for members of the LGBTQ+ community have appeared. This is a trend that will likely continue as stories of LGBTQ+ people become more mainstream.

Chapter 3 is all about identity—who we are and how we present ourselves to others at certain times and in certain places. It takes courage to be yourself, especially when we are all constantly growing and changing. The stories and sources shared in chapter 3 show that no person is static or simply defined. Being true to yourself is an important step in creating change.

Chapter 4 builds on the idea of knowing who you are so that you can find a community. The solidarity a community provides is important for any individual's well-being and, in some cases, it's crucial for the progress of society.

Chapter 5 chronicles just some of the many ways that people choose to get active and take a stand.

Appendix A presents a map of Wisconsin displaying the locations of the people, organizations, and events featured in this book.

Appendix B provides a timeline of historic LGBTQ+ events related to each source in the book.

Appendix C lists many additional resources—like books, websites, and magazine articles—where you can learn more about these topics!

We, the authors, feel a great respect for all of the people whose stories we've shared in this book. We thank them for their sacrifices, bravery, and actions, knowing that those of us who walk in their footsteps have a slightly easier path. Together, we will walk on in their legacy, forging a better path for those to come, because we will always be here.

1

Educate Yourself

(Because Knowledge Is Power)

What we learn shapes us into the people we become. We are taught by our teachers, families, and friends, but we must also take our education into our own hands and seek out topics that matter to us. This is especially true of topics that don't normally come up in classrooms or in casual conversations.

For many years, books, magazines, TV shows, and other works that include LGBTQ+ material have been banned by authorities like libraries, schools, religious groups, and even the federal government. Until relatively recently, it has been difficult for LGBTQ+ people in America to see themselves reflected in literature and other forms of media. The first time homosexuality entered the mainstream public media in Wisconsin was in 1895 during the London trials of the well-known author Oscar Wilde. Sadly, the newspaper accounts of Wilde as a gay man were far from flattering.[1]

Luckily, it is easier to find information on any subject today than it was in 1895. And there are more works that feature LGBTQ+ people and issues in the mainstream media than ever before! Still, each media outlet presents things differently. It's up to you to think carefully about where you're getting your information.

The simple act of reading about people like you can be incredibly powerful. The following sources demonstrate how information

The Irish poet and playwright Oscar Wilde, pictured here around 1882, was convicted of "gross indecency" for his romantic relationships with men. LIBRARY OF CONGRESS #98519699

about the LGBTQ+ community can awaken, educate, and inspire in different ways. We hope they motivate you to seek out new reading materials for yourself!

"Female Impersonator" Advertisement

Sometimes we learn as much from advertisements as we do from any other reading material. In the 1960s, it would have been rare to see LGBTQ+ folks mentioned in mainstream media outlets. But Adrian Ames graced the pages of many local Wisconsin newspapers in advertisements for his shows as a "female impersonator."

Ames performed throughout Wisconsin in the 1950s and 1960s. The shows mentioned in the ad on the following page took place over ten nights in Sheboygan on the last days of 1960 and the first days of 1961. Ames was flamboyant and fabulous. He often sent press releases to newspapers to brag about the tens of thousands of dollars he'd spent on wardrobe and jewelry for performances.[2]

Female impersonators or drag queens have long provided a visual and cultural representation for anyone wishing to enact gender nonconformity. Attending one of Ames's shows was a popular and mostly positive way to see what someone switching genders might look like, even if that's not how his show was billed. If you were an LGBTQ+ teenager in Sheboygan in 1960, you would have found very few outlets for learning about queer or gender-nonconforming people. How would you have reacted to this ad about a man who dressed as a flashy woman to perform for adoring audiences? Would it have had an impact on your understanding of your own gender?

Advertisement featuring Adrian Ames in the
Sheboygan Daily Press, **December 30, 1960**

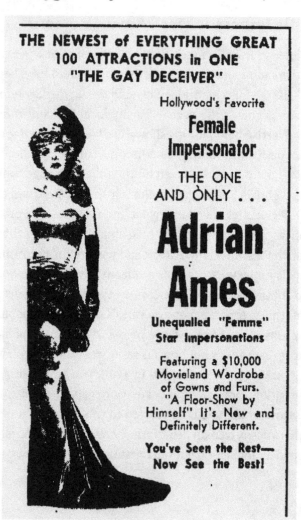

NEWSPAPERARCHIVE

GPU News

One way to learn more about LGBTQ+ issues is by reading materials created by local and regional LGBTQ+ groups and organizations. Today, you might try visiting websites or finding groups on social media. In the early 1970s, organizations such as the Gay People's Union (GPU) in Milwaukee printed and distributed their own newspapers, as some groups still do today.

> I like this source because I think it is important for others to see the struggles people face because of their sexual orientation.

Founded by UW–Milwaukee students in 1971, the GPU was an incredibly important LGBTQ+ group in Wisconsin. Five individuals printed their names on the board of directors list when the

Editor Eldon Murray (left) and other volunteers produced *GPU News* using typewriters, glue, staplers, and other supplies in this office in Milwaukee. ARCHIVES DEPARTMENT, UNIVERSITY OF WISCONSIN–MILWAUKEE LIBRARIES

GPU's articles of incorporation were filed—Gerald Earl Meyers, Michael Mitchell, Eldon Murray, Louis Stimac, and Donna Utke. The seemingly simple act of making their names public was courageous because state laws still viewed homosexuality as a criminal offense. As the group became official, lawyers tried to charge them more, banks did not allow them to open accounts, and the federal government refused to recognize them multiple times.[3]

The GPU sent speakers into Milwaukee's community, hosted conventions, organized dances, and opened a health clinic, among other initiatives. For a few years, the GPU sponsored the radio program *Gay Perspective*.[4] It was one of the country's first regularly scheduled gay radio programs.[5] The group also published the monthly newspaper *GPU News* for about a decade. As you can read in the article below, the paper was distributed by GPU members. People were encouraged to pass issues along to friends. The editors also relied on readers to provide content for their issues. Like so many early LGBTQ+ publications, *GPU News* was a do-it-yourself project and a labor of love.

• • • • • • • • • • • • • •

"GPU Publishes New Newspaper" in *GPU News*, October 1971

After several issues of a mimeographed newsletter called "Take Heed," Gay Peoples Union is proud to present a new format for our newspaper. We are not too happy with the name of this newspaper, but could not decide on one that was neither corny nor too camp. If you have any suggestions for a better name, please send them to us for consideration.

We expect to publish monthly, but if we are to achieve this goal, we will need help. A great deal of effort by a few non-journalistic people have made this paper possible. If you have journalistic talents, typing

ARCHIVES DEPARTMENT, UNIVERSITY OF WISCONSIN–MILWAUKEE LIBRARIES

abilities, artistic abilities, or writing abilities, please volunteer your services for future issues.

In order to make the newspaper represent the views of the entire gay community, we would appreciate your comments and suggestions for articles. We hope to act as a news gathering service for the gay community. If you will report to us any local or even national news item, it will help us to make the paper newsworthy. In this issue you will see a column called "Homosexuality in the Media." If you see or hear homosexuality discussed on television, radio, newspaper, or in magazines, please note the source and call [555-5555].

Paid advertising supports all newspapers and ours is no exception.

Contact us for our advertising rates. We reserve the right to edit or refuse advertising. We will not accept ads which solicit. After all, GPU is not a dating or mating service. While we are talking about advertising, we hope that you will tell the establishments that you have seen their ad in *GPU News*. It goes without saying that you should support those businesses which help GPU.

This issue is being distributed by GPU members who are asking for a small donation for each copy. At the present time we have no set-up for subscriptions, but expect to announce mail subscription rates in the near future. It is our hope that this paper will soon achieve circulation outside the Milwaukee area. After you have read this issue why not pass it along to a friend?

Our Lives Magazine

Regional newspapers share news with subscribers in and around specific cities, like *GPU News* did for Milwaukee. State-focused LGBTQ+ magazines like *Our Lives* publish articles, interviews, stories, and other pieces specifically by, for, and featuring Wisconsinites.

Our Lives is a bimonthly LGBTQ+ magazine that was founded in Madison in 2009. As the editors stated in an early issue, "Our goal is to deliver each story, identity and person regardless of notoriety or lack thereof. We aim to demonstrate how we overcome obstacles on a day-to-day basis. The progress our community has made is undeniable and the applause deserved is what we intend to provide."[6] *Our Lives* runs news stories, profiles notable individuals, and even includes job listings. The website also provides news coverage, a calendar of events, and a photo gallery. Just as early LGBTQ+ magazines did in the 1950s, *Our Lives* strives to create a welcoming community for its readers.

our lives

36

44

Johannes
Wollmann

Madison's LGBT&XYZ Magazine

ENTERTAINMENT

Local experts share the best in arts & culture

bringing

CUBA

to MADISON

Ricardo Gonzalez
cardinal bar owner

September/October 2015

OURLIVESMADISON.COM ›› Connect Our Community ›› **FACEBOOK.COM/OURLIVESMAGAZINE**

Ricardo Gonzalez on the cover of the September/October 2015 issue of *Our Lives*.
COURTESY OF *OUR LIVES*

The following is an excerpt from a personal essay by Ricardo Gonzalez, a Cuban immigrant, iconic Madison bar owner, and local politician. It's a good example of how *Our Lives* aims to amplify and applaud the stories of unique LGBTQ+ individuals in Wisconsin.

⬤⬤⬤⬤⬤⬤⬤⬤⬤⬤⬤⬤⬤
⬤⬤⬤⬤⬤⬤⬤⬤⬤⬤⬤⬤⬤⬤

Excerpt from "Cuban, Libre" by Ricardo Gonzalez in *Our Lives*, September/October 2015

They all gasped when they saw me coming into the living room wearing my mother's evening gown and high heels. After all, I was only five and it wasn't the sort of thing a boy would do, but the dress lay on her bed and I instinctively put it on, slipped into the shoes and out I paraded in front of company no less! To this day my older brothers remember the scene and kid me about it, realizing that it wasn't just mischievousness, but the first sign of my being different.

Growing up in Cuba, especially in Camaguey—one of the island's most conservative areas—middle class boys did not grow up to be dancers, actors or artists, let alone drag queens; yet that was what I wanted to be until the realization hit me that if I pursued those dreams I would

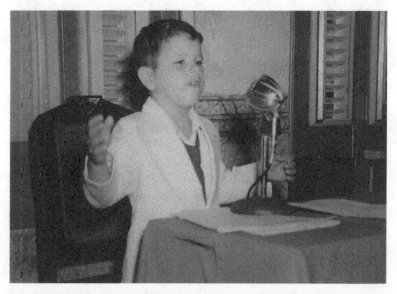

This picture of Ricardo Gonzalez reciting a poem at his school in Cuba was taken when he was five years old. COURTESY OF RICARDO GONZALEZ

COURTESY OF *OUR LIVES*

be called a maricon [a derogatory Spanish term for a gay man] and I knew that was bad. So then I took refuge in the Church, becoming an altar boy and announcing to my parents that I wanted to be a Marist brother [a member of a Catholic institute known as the Marist Brothers]. I must have been about 10 or 11, and their response was to wait and see how I felt about it in a few years. But by the time I was 13, all I wanted to do was dance and party.

We grew into a young adulthood rather fast. The drinking age in Cuba may have been 16 or 18, but no one paid attention. A boy, especially, would start drinking whenever he wanted. For me and my friends that happened around age 13; we would go to parties at someone's home or at the social club and there would be rum and cokes—and dancing! There wasn't any dating as such, but we were already thinking about girls. Being a social butterfly, I had to have a girlfriend and so began courting. Never mind that my fantasies were all about my boyfriends, I would learn to keep those deeply buried and carry on with the charade of being the Latin lover until finally coming out at 22.

"Two Black Women Seek Marriage License" in *The Ladder*

Nationally distributed LGBTQ+ newspapers and magazines provide information from outside one's local or statewide community. While *GPU News* was circulated by hand mostly around Milwaukee in the early 1970s, a few national LGBTQ+ publications launched as early as the 1950s.

Manonia Evans (left) was twenty-one years old and Donna Burkett (right) was twenty-five when they applied for a marriage license in Milwaukee in 1971. © USA TODAY NETWORK

The *Ladder*, produced in California, was the first nationally distributed lesbian magazine in the country. When it was first printed in 1956, issues were mailed in brown paper envelopes to conceal the content.[7] The US Postal Service considered any printed information about homosexuality—even plain text—to be "indecent." But the women who read *The Ladder* were hungry for connection and for information about each other. *The Ladder* printed stories submitted from people across the nation, including Wisconsin.

In 1972, the magazine ran a small news item with the headline: "Two Black Women Seek Marriage License." Donna Burkett and Manonia Evans of Milwaukee argued that they were missing out on tax benefits by not being allowed to marry.[8] They eventually lost their court case and were not able to legally marry, but they did have a church ceremony. That brief article in *The Ladder* surely had a profound impact on many of the magazine's readers (by 1972, it had nearly 4,000 subscribers). Some of those readers may have remembered that article forty-four years later, in 2015, when same-sex marriage finally became legal in all fifty states.

• • • • • • • • • • • • •

"Two Black Women Seek Marriage License" in *The Ladder*, February/March 1972

> TWO BLACK WOMEN SEEK MARRIAGE LICENSE: Milwaukee, October, 1971. Donna Burkett, 25, and Manonia Evans, 21, have filed suit in U.S. District Court in Milwaukee in an effort to obtain a marriage license. The couple said (among other things) that they were "being deprived of marital benefits such as inheritance rights and the filing of a joint income tax return".

LYSISTRATA AND LESBIAN EPHEMERA COLLECTION, BOX 1, UNIVERSITY OF WISCONSIN–MADISON ARCHIVES, MADISON, WISCONSIN

• • • • • • • • • • • • •

The Queer Zine Archive Project

Like *GPU News* earlier in this chapter, many LGBTQ+ publications are distributed through underground channels. Of all the different kinds of publications, though, zines may be the most underground. Most zines are homemade and feature alternative topics. They are usually passed around by hand, from friend to friend, popping up one minute and disappearing the next. So, how do you find material like this if you do not know where to look? The Queer Zine Ar-

> *The Queer Zine Archive Project gives us a chance to find easily accessible stories and support creators.*

chive Project hoped to provide an answer to this question when it launched in Milwaukee in 2003. The project's website states:

> The mission of the Queer Zine Archive Project (QZAP) is to establish a "living history" archive of past and present queer zines and to encourage current and emerging zine publishers to continue to create. In curating such a unique aspect of culture, we value a collectivist approach that respects the diversity of experiences that fall under the heading "queer."
>
> The primary function of QZAP is to provide a free on-line searchable database of the collection with links allowing users to view or download electronic copies of zines. By providing access to the historical canon of queer zines we hope to make them more accessible to diverse communities and reach wider audiences.[9]

This 2007 issue of *Mxd Zine*, held in the Queer Zine Archive Project's collections, focuses on the experiences of mixed-race people and issues of gender identity. THE QUEER ZINE ARCHIVE PROJECT

Milo Miller and Chris Wilde run the archive—a collection of more than 2,500 zines from across the globe. Six hundred of the zines are available for viewing online, and the hard copies are stored in Miller and Wilde's basement in Milwaukee.[10] Some of the zines focus on teaching self-defense, others are dedicated to specific kinds of music from punk to Bruce Springsteen, and others are simply coloring books. Zines like these were created for communities outside the mainstream. They help LGBTQ+ people with various interests and passions connect with others like them. As Miller told the *Milwaukee Journal Sentinel* in 2018, "We're trying to preserve history and voices, and we're trying to promote them."[11]

One of the Milwaukee-based zines in the QZAP collection is *Life Has a Beard* by Basil Beardsley. Published in 2007, the zine contains an assortment of thoughts, poems, and links to content about high school, environmentalism, television, and other topics. There is only one volume of this zine in the archive. Many zines are created as unique single issues. Why do you think young LGBTQ+ people might be drawn to zines like the one featured below rather than commercial media like newspapers or magazines?

• • • • • • • • • • • • •

"Carnival" in *Life Has a Beard*
by Basil Beardsley, 2007

"Burn it down, nothing left, everybody, fun 'til death!"

We were running and we were screaming and we were dancing in the streets. A purple-haired woman strode past on stilts, her ruffled dress sweeping behind. A fairy prince (wings and all) rode past upon his bicycle with every potential for flight. A militant, torch-bearing, dress-wearing lumberjack of a unicyclist wove amidst the crowd.

We were maniacs, two hundred strong. It was a guerilla-dance-party street-reclamation. It was a cacophony of acrobats swinging from street lights, of children-in-age and children-at-heart singing and chanting, of

THE QUEER ZINE ARCHIVE PROJECT

the rhythmic thudding of dancing feet upon the road and celebratory drumming upon dumpsters and other make-shift musical instruments, of obstructed motorists blaring their horns in impatient anger (or was it desire?) A lone didgeridoo wailed amidst the throngs. The spectacle disintegrated as one-by-one the spectators fell victim to tempting osmosis into the teeming mass of fire-dancers and brick-throwers and costume-clad lunatics; as they fell victim to the lure of our riotous celebration of life itself.

Even as the pepper-spray and tear gas canisters came raining down, our collective ecstatic (or was it orgasmic?) adrenaline rush lead us away; lead us to shelter and barricades and babies too overwhelmed to cry; to showers to rinse our burning faces; to play hide and seek with the police; to sing of insurrection another day.

• • • • • • • • • • •

Educate Yourself

You can educate yourself on any topic—even ones that don't appear in your textbooks or on the shelves of your library. Members of the LGBTQ+ community have learned about others like themselves by reading written works like the ones in this chapter. You can choose to get your information from a wide variety of sources, all of which communicate different stories and perspectives. Analyze the information you consume just as you analyze the sources in this book. And, remember, knowledge is power.

2

Tell Your Story

(Because No One Else Can)

Educating yourself with accurate and interesting information about LGBTQ+ issues is an important element of activism. And telling your story, or the stories of others, is one way to extend your activist efforts beyond yourself.

There are many ways to be a storyteller. Some people write about their personal experiences in poems, articles, essays, and memoirs. Some use their experiences as inspiration for fictional characters in short stories and novels. Still more document the stories of their communities through journalism and nonfiction books. And writing is not the only way to tell a story. Narratives can be expressed through the spoken word as oral histories and interviews or through visual art, dance, music, and more.

Telling your own stories can be uncomfortable. It can be terrifying to share yourself with others who may react to or interpret your words differently than you imagined. But each of the storytellers in this book faced similar fears. Whether you would like to tell your own story or the stories of your community, we hope you find inspiration in the examples included in this chapter. After reading them, reflect on a story you'd like to tell and give it a try!

Lou Sullivan's Diary Entries

Telling your story can start with reflections in a journal or diary. Lou Sullivan was a transgender gay man born in Wauwatosa, Wisconsin, in 1951. During his youth, he dreamed of becoming a writer. At the age of eleven,

> *This is a really cool source from a time when being transgender was even more taboo than it is now.*

he began recording his life in a pink vinyl diary. In his early journal entries, Sullivan recorded his feelings, observations, and desires. He noted that he "played boys" as an eleven year old. He explored his identity on the page long before he ever told anyone else about feeling like a man trapped in a woman's body.[1] Journaling is a very personal form of writing, and most journals are not intended to be shared. Often people who journal find it valuable to look back and reflect on the thoughts of their younger selves. Journals can act as time capsules, recording who you were and how you felt at pivotal moments in your life.

Sullivan's writing work did not end with journaling, and eventually he used his writing skills to help others. In the 1970s, he wrote articles on transgender issues and theory that were published in Milwaukee's *GPU News* (see page 23 for more information on *GPU News*). After moving to California in 1975, he began editing a female-to-male newsletter. This newsletter began one of the first trans male organizations, FTM International. In his 1980 book *Information for the Female-to-Male Crossdresser and Transsexual*, Sullivan gave advice on clothing items, hairstyles, and body language for trans men. He also included images of people assigned female at birth dressing in men's clothes throughout history.[2] In 1990, Sullivan wrote the biography of another transgender man: *From Female to Male: The Life of Jack Bee Garland*.

The diary entries on pages 38 and 39 were written when Sullivan was fifteen, sixteen, and nineteen years old, respectively. He

In 1966, fifteen-year-old Lou Sullivan experimented with adopting a masculine style. COURTESY OF GAY, LESBIAN, BISEXUAL, TRANSGENDER HISTORICAL SOCIETY

continued to keep a diary until his death from AIDS in 1991. Lou Sullivan started exploring his gender and sexuality by writing in a diary, and he ended up becoming one of the first publicly gay trans men to medically transition. In 2007, FTM International dedicated an entire issue of its newsletter to his life and the impact he had on others.

• • • • • • • • • • • •
• • • • • • • • • • • •

Diary entry by Lou Sullivan, June 6, 1966

I want to look like what I am but don't know what some one like me looks like. I mean, when people look at me, I want them to think—there's one of those people . . . that has their own interpretation of happiness. That's what I am.

Diary entry by Lou Sullivan, March 10, 1967

I thought of the days when I really thought I was a cowboy. I dressed the part and really was one. I don't have to dress up any more and I'm glad. The cowboy's in my soul, where he counts. He doesn't have a name because he's a thousand different men. Always men though. I really should have been a boy. I'd've been so much happier as a boy. I'll probably make a good marriage 'cause my husband'll be me in all I want for myself. I'll treat him as though he were me. Strange.

Lou Sullivan recorded his thoughts in this diary in 1980, when he was in his late twenties. COURTESY OF GAY, LESBIAN, BISEXUAL, TRANSGENDER HISTORICAL SOCIETY

Diary entry by Lou Sullivan, November 22, 1970

My heart and soul is with the drag queens. This last week or so I've wanted to go and leave everything and join that world. But where do I fit in? I feel so deprived and sad and lost. What can become of a girl whose real desire and passion is with male homosexuals? That I want to be one? I still yearn for that world, that world I know nothing about, a serious, threatening, sad, ferocious, stormy, lost world.

● ● ● ● ● ● ● ● ● ● ● ● ●

Glenway Wescott's Short Stories

> I was surprised to see so many early stories, like this one, of people being relatively open.

While Lou Sullivan recorded his feelings and experiences in a diary, some storytellers take bits and pieces of their personal stories and turn them into fiction. Glenway Wescott is one of the early gay authors who called Wisconsin home. In his book *Good-Bye, Wisconsin*, he wrote short stories about fictional characters growing up and leaving Wisconsin.

Wescott was born in Kewaskum, Wisconsin, in 1901. He attended West Bend High School and discovered his homosexuality during that time.[3] His writing career truly began in 1924 with the publication of his novel *The Apple of the Eye*. Wescott then published two books that reflected his Wisconsin roots: *The Grandmothers* in 1927 and *Good-Bye, Wisconsin* in 1928. These publications earned him some fame, but Wescott felt he could not stay in Wisconsin. In his writings, he claimed the Midwest was a nice place to grow up—a statement still made by many people today. But Wescott ultimately felt that Wisconsin did not accept who he became. On visits back, he reflected on the "provincial" nature of the people.

Glenway Wescott posed for this photograph in France in 1927, one year before the publication of his book *Good-Bye, Wisconsin*. COURTESY OF THE ESTATE OF GLENWAY WESCOTT

In New York and Paris, Wescott found the accepting and vibrant community he could not find in his home state. He went on to spend time with well-known gay writers throughout his life, such as Gertrude Stein, Thornton Wilder, and Jean Cocteau.

The excerpt on the following page is from the short story "Adolescence" in his book *Good-Bye, Wisconsin*. Wescott was likely inspired by a real experience in his life. With the help of another teenaged boy, Wescott once dressed up as a girl for a masked dance in high school.[4] As you read the following excerpt, imagine how Wescott may have used his real-life experience to write his short story. Can you think of a story from your life that you could turn into a piece of fiction? How might fictionalizing your story affect the way other people read and respond to it?

● ● ● ● ● ● ● ● ● ● ● ●

Excerpt from "Adolescence" in *Good-Bye, Wisconsin* by Glenway Wescott, 1928

In the attic bedroom of a large house at twilight two youngsters were trying to make up their minds about a masquerade party. Out of the stairway rose an agreeable odor of bath-towels and tobacco and face-powder, reminding the younger boy of his friend's brothers and fashionable mother, whom he admired but who often embarrassed him. He came from the country, and was sensuous and timid.

Carl, who was at home there, was the youngest of the four sons of one of three brothers who owned the flour-mill and several stores and a number of houses in the town. Philip had only his father and mother, and they were poor. [The boys] were respectively fifteen and thirteen years old. . . .

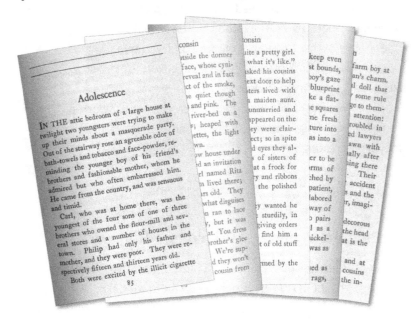

HARPER & BROTHERS

It was from the bulky yellow house under the elms that they had received an invitation to a fancy-dress party. A girl named Rita who went to school with them lived there; she was going to be fifteen years old. They could not make up their minds what disguises to adopt. Philip's imagination ran to lace curtains and borrowed jewelry, but it was Carl who said: "I'll tell you what. You dress up as a woman. I'll get my brother's glee club suit and wear a mustache. We're supposed to wear masks, anyway, and they won't know you and I'll say you're my cousin from Milwaukee. You'll make quite a pretty girl. Just for the fun of it. See what it's like."

The next afternoon they asked his cousins Lucy and Lois in the house next door to help them.... As Carl explained what they wanted he leaned against the mantelpiece sturdily, in imitation of his elder brothers giving orders to indulgent women. "You'll find him a dress, won't you? You have a lot of old stuff in the cherry cupboard."...

[Philip] came there again two days later to be tormented by one of the worst forms of fatigue, that of erect immobility touched by many nervous hands, pinched and patient, measured, turned about, discussed, labored over. They stood him on a stool by way of a pedestal. The sharp mouths of two pairs of scissors played about him, as well as a quiverful of pins both black and nickel-plated, often piercing to the skin. He was as happy and nervous as a young martyr.

The excitement of the sisters increased as they worked. Out of some bright old rags, pins, coral beads, and a boy—a farm boy at that— they were creating a woman's charm.

* * * * * * * * * * * * *

R. Richard Wagner's Wisconsin History

Telling the stories of members of your community is another way to share the LGBTQ+ experience. R. Richard "Dick" Wagner of Madison has dedicated much of his adult life to writing about the LGBTQ+ history of Wisconsin. Over the years, he has sought

out and saved materials important to preserving this history—
everything from postcards, photographs, and scrapbooks to newspaper articles, meeting notes, and magazine advertisements. He
currently has more than forty boxes of these materials in what he
calls his "gay archive."

Wagner was the first openly gay man to serve on the Dane
County Board of Supervisors (see page 102 to learn about the later
actions of Wagner and two other out Dane County supervisors).
And in 1983, he was appointed co-chair of the Governor's Council on Gay and Lesbian Issues, traveling across Wisconsin to learn
about LGBTQ+ communities across the state. Collecting materials throughout his life meant that when he sat down to write his
two-volume gay history of Wisconsin—*We've Been Here All Along:
Wisconsin's Early Gay History* and *Coming Out, Moving Forward:
Wisconsin's Recent Gay History*—he had access to stories no one
else did. These two books form the foundation of the one you are
reading now.

R. Richard Wagner's two volumes of Wisconsin's gay history. WISCONSIN
HISTORICAL SOCIETY PRESS

Wagner explained to us as we wrote this book:

> The reason I write is not because I enjoy writing but because I wish to share stories that I think are important. This stems from having learned to enjoy stories from reading them. . . . I found enjoyment in reading and further should admit what I can see now: it was an escape into books. The escape was comforting because even then as a proto-gay kid I felt I did not quite fit into the "normal" mode. I also threw myself into my school lessons. . . . Besides, knowledge appealed as a reward. I would play mind games with friends like naming the capitals of all the European countries or the American states. But in those days I was not seeing myself as a writer.[5]

In an interview with the *Capital Times* in 2016, Wagner acknowledged that writing about history has helped him learn about himself:

> Many people who were raised as I was in the 1950s, we had no information about homosexuality. . . . And so, one, I had to figure it out. And two, I had to find real information, so the discovery of that information sort of becomes a lifelong task when one doesn't have resources.[6]

The following excerpt from the introduction of *Coming Out, Moving Forward* provides more details about Wagner's two volumes on Wisconsin's gay history.

• • • • • • • • • • • • •

Excerpt from *Coming Out, Moving Forward*
by R. Richard Wagner, 2020

In *We've Been Here All Along: Wisconsin's Early Gay History*, I outlined the repressive nature of Wisconsin's laws and societal attitudes regarding homosexuality in the pre-Stonewall period. Nevertheless, some small number of gays, lesbians, and other gender nonconforming individuals found ways to emancipate themselves from these strictures during this era. They developed and presented their identities and built social networks to support one another. With incredible conviction, they faced the headwinds of dissent and persisted toward the goal of equality.

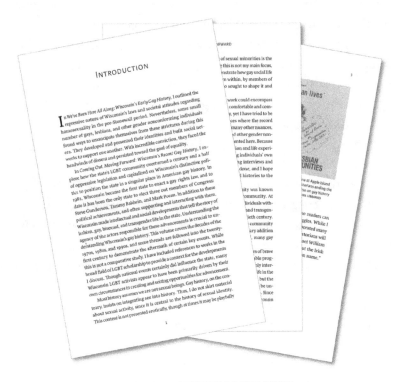

In *Coming Out, Moving Forward: Wisconsin's Recent Gay History*, I explore how the state's LGBT community overturned a century and a half of oppressive legislation and capitalized on Wisconsin's distinctive politics to position the state in a singular place in American gay history. In 1982, Wisconsin became the first state to enact a gay rights law, and to date it has been the only state to elect three out members of Congress: Steve Gunderson, Tammy Baldwin, and Mark Pocan. In addition to these political achievements, and often supporting and interacting with them, Wisconsin made intellectual and social developments that tell the story of lesbian, gay, bisexual, and transgender life in the state. Understanding the agency of the actors responsible for these advancements is crucial to understanding Wisconsin's gay history. This volume covers the decades of the 1970s, 1980s, and 1990s, and some threads are followed into the twenty-first century to demonstrate the aftermath of certain key events. While this is not a comparative study, I have included references to works in the broad field of LGBT scholarship to provide a context for the developments I discuss. Though national events certainly did influence the state, many Wisconsin LGBT activists appear to have been primarily driven by their own circumstances in creating and seizing opportunities for advancement.

The story of Wisconsin's recent gay history centers on a series of brave individuals who, with very meager resources, achieved remarkable progress in the realm of gay rights. They did this by actively and openly interacting with major institutions and changing the stories about gay life in the state. Similar developments occurred in a handful of other states, but the story of the upper Midwest, and particularly Wisconsin, needs to be understood and added to the more well-known histories of the coasts. Since LGBT voices have been so marginalized in our history—both in Wisconsin and in the nation—I have tried to bring them to the fore so readers can appreciate the personal significance of their lives and struggles. While I was not able to include as many stories as I'd like, I have incorporated many pioneer voices and names. It is my sincere hope that other historians will take on the research and writing of more of this history. As poet William Butler Yeats wrote in his momentous poem "Easter 1916" about the Irish rebellion of that year, it is now "our part to murmur name upon name."

Newsletters and *Leaping La Crosse News*

Another way some people share LGBTQ+ stories is through newsletters—communications sent to specific groups of subscribers or community members. *Leaping La Crosse News* (*LLN*) did not have a fancy format or structure, but it was an important publication that amplified the voices of lesbians in western Wisconsin. The newsletter printed over three hundred issues between 1978 and 2007. They are now held at UW–La Crosse's Murphy Library and entirely accessible online. *LLN* started as the newsletter of the National Lesbian Feminist Organization. You can see the organization's acronym, NLFO, in the upper right corner of the newsletter on the next page. After fifteen issues, the name changed to *Leaping La Crosse News*.

Designed to share news, advertise gatherings, and connect community members, the newsletter covered everything from music festivals to birth announcements. *LLN*'s major goal was to provide a safe and encouraging space for the lesbian population of western Wisconsin. The article on the following page captures *LLN*'s response to an important "coming out" moment for its readers: the January 1981 broadcast of a five-part special report on La Crosse's gay community by WLCX, a local radio station.

Though it is no longer being published, *LLN* was an important and long-standing source of information, entertainment, and connection for many lesbians in the La Crosse area. It is just one of many LGBTQ+ newsletters that have been created, printed, and distributed in Wisconsin and around the nation. *Among Friends*, *Gay Madison*, *Hag Rag*, and other newsletters have similarly demonstrated the presence of LGBTQ+ people in communities that might not have previously recognized them. If you were an LGBTQ+ person living in La Crosse in 1981, how would you have reacted to a radio station broadcasting a special report about you and your community? Do you think this would have impacted your view of yourself?

• • • • • • • • • • • • •

"Yes La Crosse, WE ARE HERE!"
in *Leaping La Crosse News*, January 1981

COURTESY OF MURPHY LIBRARY DIGITAL COLLECTIONS,
UNIVERSITY OF WISCONSIN–LA CROSSE

So now we're famous!!! Does it feel any different? . . . NOT YET . . . and we hope it stays that way!!

In mid-January WLCX decided to do a five part special report on La Crosse's Gay Community. They were VERY positive in their approach and gave a very honest and supportive presentation. THANKS WLCX!!

The concern within the gay community comes in when La Crosse finally realizes . . . WE ARE HERE!!! Until recently, most people in La Crosse had no idea of the size of the gay community . . . now they do! Hopefully they will come to a positive understanding and not strike out against us as "God's Country's Moral Majority." But . . . chances are, there will be some negative feedback. So, keep your eyes and ears open . . . if we hear or see any inklings, let's get them out in the open right away so we know what we're up against!

* * * * * * * * * * * * * *

The Digital Transgender Archive's Oral Histories

Some stories are spoken aloud rather than being written down. An oral history is typically an interview that is saved as an audio or video recording and shared through an archive.[7] Archives keep papers, materials, recordings, and artifacts so that they can be discovered again and again by students throughout history. The Digital Transgender Archive is entirely online; it links to artifacts and oral histories held at institutions throughout the country. The archive features many oral histories with transgender folks of color, such as Selena Meza, who recorded their interview as part of the Tretter Transgender Oral History Project.

Selena identifies as a Mexican American queer trans femme assigned male at birth and uses both they/them and she/her pronouns. They're originally from Chicago, Illinois, and moved to rural Nekoosa, Wisconsin, when they were around five years old. The Digital Transgender Archive has many recordings of stories like

This photo of Selena Meza was taken during their oral history interview for the Tretter Transgender Oral History Project in 2017 in Minneapolis, Minnesota.
COURTESY OF THE TRETTER TRANSGENDER ORAL HISTORY PROJECT

Selena's. Why is Selena's voice and story important to capture in an oral history? How could your story add to our understanding of Wisconsin history?

Excerpt from "Interview with Selena Meza" in the Tretter Transgender Oral History Project, November 19, 2017

The first time I ever met a trans person . . . the first time I actually ever seen a trans person was probably when I was like 10 years old and . . . my brother would do a paper route. . . . I remember there was a trans person that was also doing the paper route. He would kind of make fun of her, because back in the day that was just something that you never saw. It was bizarre and something that you would pick at and that's what my brother was doing. I just remember . . . I remember that person because they would be there all the time and dress fabulous just doing the paper route. . . .

Kids now are really cool. My nephews and nieces, when they talk to me about being trans, they just are really open-minded to it already, and I like that about the youth right now, that they really seem to be open-minded to it. I think that they're not going to have as hard of a time when it comes to the future of gender identity and hopefully that's right, where they can just be themselves and not have to put a label to it. There's where I kind of struggle with labels is in the trans community where we have to label a lot of things. That's also kind of conforming to cis normatives and that's something that I struggle with because I don't want to conform to them, to be cis normative, the construct, because being trans you're not going to be accepted in the society that was made for cis people—white cis people. So, I think that's something that I was struggling with at first, just like, I don't want to conform to just being this female, what you think a female is.

Telling Your Story

Telling your story, or the stories of others in your community, is an excellent way to ensure that LGBTQ+ history will not be forgotten. Stories can be educational, thought-provoking, or simply fun. What stories can you tell about your life or the lives of others? Telling stories in your own words is important, because no one else can tell your story like you can.

3

Be True to Yourself

(Because Self-Acceptance Is Key)

Each one of us brings something unique to this world. Dressing and acting as yourself, having relationships with whomever you choose, pursuing the jobs you want and the passions you love—these are things that make the world a richer place. However, these are freedoms that US law and mainstream society have denied to LGBTQ+ people throughout much of history. Many individuals have been emotionally traumatized and physically harmed simply for being themselves. Yet there are many historical examples of LGBTQ+ folks who found creative and inspiring ways to be true to their identities, even in very challenging situations.

We can never truly know what it feels like to be someone else. But as you read the primary sources in this chapter, we challenge you to try seeing the world through another person's eyes. Imagine how you might have felt in their shoes. We hope these stories embolden you to take action by expressing your own identity. Sometimes, being true to yourself is the most courageous thing you can do!

Ralph Kerwineo: Early Cross-Dresser

In 1914, Ralph Kerwineo was arrested in Milwaukee for disorderly conduct. He was working at the Cutler-Hammer Electrical Equipment factory storeroom. Ralph's long-term girlfriend had gone to the police and accused him of being a biological female. Cross-dressing was illegal at the time.[1]

Ralph had begun cross-dressing in private. He ventured into public after he realized he could make more money and earn more respect if people believed he was a man. At the time of his trial, he reflected, "I convinced myself in my own mind that I was a man. I thought of myself as a man.

> This is a fascinating story about a young trans man in 1914 and how court deals with him.

As a girl I used to love pretty dresses and the pretty trinkets that all girls prize. As a young man, I put aside these things. I learned to smoke and I found enjoyment in the pleasures of men."[2] Ralph had spent years living with a woman named Mamie White, but then he met another young woman named Dorothy Kleinowsky. Dorothy and Ralph had a whirlwind romance and married quickly with a license obtained by the city of Milwaukee.

Mamie was unhappy and began to expose Ralph's biological sex by talking to his superiors at Cutler-Hammer. She spoke to Dorothy's mother and then to the district attorney to claim spousal abandonment.[3] Soon, Ralph was arrested. When his family in Indiana found out about the charges, they were convinced that he had been hypnotized.

The article from the *Milwaukee Sentinel* on page 56 uses alternate spellings of Ralph's and Dorothy's last names, and it uses offensive language to describe Ralph's gender identity and race (he was the child of an African American father and a Potawatomi mother).[4] It also demonstrates the rigid gender roles of the time.

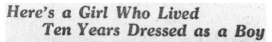

Ralph Kerwineo lived in Milwaukee for about eight years before he was arrested for disorderly conduct and forced to present himself as a woman. *MILWAUKEE SENTINEL*

Can you imagine what it would feel like for a judge to rule that you must wear certain clothing items and not others?

Ralph was forced to return to using his birth name, and he lived out the rest of his days as a woman in Milwaukee and Chicago. After the case, he remarked "My heart and soul are more those of a man than a woman."[5]

• • • • • • • • • • • • • •
• • • • • • • • • • • • •

"Throngs in Court to See 'Girl-Man;' Case is Continued" in the *Milwaukee Sentinel*, May 4, 1914

Enjoying the notoriety she created, Cora Anderson, alias Ralph Kerwineio, who deceived her associates ten years masquerading as a boy, was arraigned in District court on Monday, charged with disorderly conduct, and a continuance of her case granted to May 7, on application of Attorney Thomas E. Leahy.

A huge throng watched her entrance into the courtroom. Hundreds of curious persons lined the sidewalks on Oneida street, between the police station and the city hall for hours on Monday waiting until the little dark skinned girl-boy should put in an appearance.

After her arraignment she was closeted with the district attorney, her counsel and the county clerk, Louis G. Widule, for half an hour. Later the district attorney said Cora would be sent out with Mrs. Jordan, complaint clerk, to obtain suitable clothes for a woman.

Dr. Harry Bradley, before a postponement of her case was taken, testified that he made a partial examination of the former bellhop. He said she was normal and exceptionally bright.

MILWAUKEE SENTINEL,
MAY 4, 1914

What action if any will be taken against the west side physician who issued the health certificate for the masquerader's wedding has not been officially announced. The girl readily assented to donning girl's attire when the request was put to her in mandatory form. Not having worn the skirts of woman in over ten years the change will be a novelty.

Cora Anderson, alias Ralph Kerwineio, obtained a license certificate at the county courthouse on March 19. According to License Clerk Frank Goreki, a certificate of health was presented purporting to have been issued by Dr. William J. Scollard. "Mr." Kerwineio gave "his" age as 25 and the space on the license duplicate declared that the applicant was of dark complexion. The occupation was given as clerk and the birthplace as South America. The name of the prospective "bride" was given as Dorothy Kleinowski, 476 Oakland Avenue, and the age as 21.

Bob Neal and Edgar Hellum: Business and Life Partners

A few decades later, in rural Wisconsin, two men went into business together so they could live life on their own terms. Robert "Bob" Neal and Edgar Hellum created a world for themselves in Mineral Point in the 1930s. They opened a renowned restaurant and worked to save the Cornish buildings and history of the area. Their historically preserved houses and built landscapes, known collectively as Pendarvis, are now a part of the Wisconsin Historical Society (WHS). But before Bob and Edgar found each other and lived together as business and life partners, they forged their own paths as gay men in the early 1900s.

Bob grew up in Mineral Point and always had an interest in interior design, art, music, and antiques. As a young man, he followed his passions to large cities, working in Chicago, New York City, and

In this photo taken around 1940, Edgar Hellum (left) and Bob Neal stand in front of Polperro, one of the buildings they restored in Mineral Point. MINERAL POINT LIBRARY ARCHIVES

London. Edgar was from Stoughton, Wisconsin. He spent his early years working in numerous places according to WHS Southwest Sites Program Manager Bethany Brander, including "a restaurant, an auto shop, two print studios, and his family's shoe and leather factory, and as a carpenter."[6] The two men met when Bob was visiting home from London and Edgar was working on a carpentry job in Mineral Point.

Below is the first known letter sent from Edgar to Bob after they met in 1934. Though we don't know the exact events of the weekend that Edgar mentions, it's clear that they had quite a lot of fun together. The following summer, Bob and Edgar bought Pendarvis House for ten dollars and embarked on an adventure that would last for decades. Both men aided the war effort when the United States entered World War II in 1941. Even after the life they built in the 1930s had changed, Bob and Edgar continued to care for one another into old age.

• • • • • • • • • • • • •

Letter from Edgar Hellum to Bob Neal, November 5, 1934

Bob Neal:

Just the name makes the past week end seem like make believe! I had a perfectly wonderful time, Bob. I do wish you were here or I were there! So follows—the grandest start of a friendship I have ever had!

You are coming over this weekend? If you don't I'm afraid it really will be—just a dream—a never to be—forgotten one!

I hope your plans can be made such that you can come on Friday evening. Expect we will have to share the evening with Gorge [Georgia Townsend]—after all she made this possible. Then we will have all Saturday and Sunday?

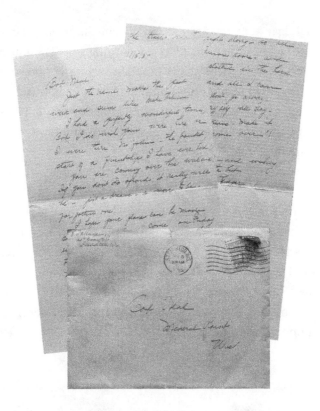

EDGAR G. HELLUM PAPERS, PENDARVIS ARCHIVES

Well we—Gorge and I arrived home O.K., after much traveling around, about 1:45 A.M. I was absolutely lost in the dark—anyway—no mishaps. The trailer rolled right along—so all the shutters—the precious doors—and the sash, are safely stacked in the barn.

I'm weary Bob—and all I can think about—please don't go away. I've kept saying it to myself all day. I do hope your plans make it possible for you to come over?!

Write—soon.

I'm thinking of you—and wishing you just the best of the best

Edgar

• • • • • • • • • • • •

Ron McCrea: Out Gay Press Chief

In contrast to Bob Neal and Edgar Hellum, who kept their romantic relationship out of the public record, Ron McCrea's sexual orientation made headlines. McCrea was a respected journalist who was out in the 1970s when there was no legal protection for LGBTQ+ people in the workforce. He was the son and grandson of newspaper professionals, and he worked for many newspapers over the course of his life, including the *Washington Post, Washington Star, Boston Globe, Capital Times, Press Connection, San Jose Mercury-News,* and *New York Newsday.*

As a well-known voice in Wisconsin's LGBTQ+ movement, McCrea participated in TV programs like *The Gay Response, Glad to Be Gay,* and *Nothing to Hide* throughout the 1970s and 1980s.[7] When he donated his collections to the LGBTQ+ Archive at UW–Madison in 2019, McCrea reflected on the newspaper article that marked the end of his public LGBTQ+ activism. He said: "My curtain call as a gay activist came when I was appointed communications director for Gov.-elect Anthony Earl in December of 1982 and the *Milwaukee Sentinel* led the paper with the headline, 'Avowed Homosexual Named Earl Press Chief.' Both Tony and I stood our ground and nobody in the media tried that again, though it may have contributed to Earl's defeat in 1986." The article, which appears on page 63, highlighted McCrea's sexual orientation over his qualifications for the job. Also, its use of the phrase "avowed homosexual" suggested that being gay was something one would only confess to with a sense of shame.[8]

When the story broke that Tony Earl (who would become governor in January 1983) had appointed an out press secretary, McCrea offered to renounce the position. However, Earl continued to support McCrea as an accomplished journalist whose role would be useful to Earl and the state. McCrea withstood bullying and badgering, and he remained press secretary throughout Earl's

Wisconsin governor-elect Tony Earl (left) appointed McCrea (right), an out gay activist, as his press secretary in 1982. PHOTO BY BRENT NICASTRO

tenure. Earl was not re-elected in 1986. The AIDS epidemic (see page 106 for more information on the HIV/AIDS epidemic) was then an international health crisis. Inaccurate and homophobic news coverage often portrayed homosexual AIDS victims as bringing the disease on themselves. Governor Earl's open support of LGBTQ+ people and AIDS victims may have prompted some people to vote against him.[9]

Romantic attraction and sexual orientation can be fluid. In 1993, McCrea married Elaine DeSmidt, and they remained married until his death in 2019.[10] McCrea didn't publicly discuss his decision to marry a woman, but writer and friend R. Richard Wagner said, "In [Ron's] later life, I heard him describe how his gay activism was necessary to protect that aspect of his sexuality but he felt no such need for his heterosexual side." McCrea continued to advocate for the LGBTQ+ community throughout his life.

Excerpt from "Avowed Homosexual Named Earl Press Chief" in the *Milwaukee Sentinel*, December 2, 1982

Gov.-Elect Anthony S. Earl Wednesday named 10 executive office appointees, including an acknowledged homosexual as his press secretary.

Ronald McCrea, 39, former editor of the defunct *Madison Press Connection* who is now working for the *San Jose (Calif.) Mercury*, will be paid $28,000 a year to run the press office and assist on policy issues and speech writing, Earl said.

McCrea had acknowledged that he is a homosexual in articles in the *Madison Press Connection*, which was published for a year after the Newspaper Guild's strike against Madison Newspapers Inc. in 1977. . . .

McCrea had worked for the *Capital Times* prior to the newspaper strike. He was first vice president of the Madison Newspaper Guild and a leading figure in the strike.

During the campaign, Earl promised he would establish a liaison with the homosexual community. Asked whether he had done so, Earl said: "No, but I still intend to keep it (the promise)."

Earl described McCrea as "a very good wordsmith . . . who will be more than someone who just composes press releases and hands them out."

McCrea, assistant national editor for the *San Jose Mercury*, said he foresees no problem with his background.

"I don't expect my personal life is going to be any kind of an issue in Wisconsin. I'm coming in to do a professional job as a professional journalist. That's all Tony asked me to do and that's all I intend to do," he said.

McCrea said he organized a gay counseling center in the early 1970s but hasn't been involved in activities in the gay community for some time.

He worked at the *Washington Post* in 1980 and the *Washington Star*

Avowed homosexual named Earl press chief

Sentinel Madison Bureau

Madison — Gov.-Elect Anthony S. Earl Wednesday named 10 executive office appointees, including an acknowledged homosexual as his press secretary.

Ronald McCrea, 39, former editor of the defunct Madison Press Connection who is now working for the San Jose (Calif.) Mercury, will be paid $28,000 a year to run the press office and assist on policy issues and speech writing, Earl said.

McCrea had acknowledged that he is a homosexual in articles in the Madison Press Connection, which was published for a year after the Newspaper Guild's strike against Madison Newspapers Inc. in 1977.

Among other appointees was Earl's campaign manager, Daniel Wisniewski, as his chief of staff. Wisniewski, 36, will be paid $46,000 a year.

He said the governor's office will be alloted 33¾ positions — the same as Gov. Dreyfus sought in his 1983-'85 budget.

Harold Bergan, 37, will be policy director at $41,500 a year. Marge Beil, 36, will run the governor's Milwaukee office and will be paid $24,000 annually.

All of the appointees were active in Earl's campaign for governor except McCrea.

McCrea had worked for The Capital Times prior to the newspaper strike. He was first vice president of the Madison Newspaper Guild and a leading figure in the strike.

During the campaign, Earl promised he would establish a liaison with the homosexual community. Asked

Turn to Page 10

Staff

MILWAUKEE SENTINEL, DECEMBER 2, 1982

in 1981. In 1980, he said, he also worked on a four-month project involving vehicle emission tests at the State Department of Natural Resources.

Earl, who was then secretary of the department, said he was impressed with McCrea's work on the project.

• • • • • • • • • • • • •

Donna Coleman: Motorcycle Club Cofounder

Motorcycle clubs for bikers who identify as women have a long and proud tradition within the LGBTQ+ community. A group of lesbians who called themselves Dykes on Bikes first led a Pride parade in San Francisco in 1976. The women rode ahead and cleared the way for floats and those on foot. In the years following, the group changed its name to the Dykes on Bikes Women's Motorcycle Contingent. They wanted to be more inclusive of all women who rode motorcycles and wished to participate. Chapters of the Women's

Donna Coleman was an avid motorcyclist. She helped found the Forker Motorcycle Club in Milwaukee to introduce other lesbians to her hobby. LIZARDS OF CENTRAL WISCONSIN PAPERS (DONNA COLEMAN), UNPROCESSED COLLECTION, DIGITAL MATERIALS, UNIVERSITY OF WISCONSIN–MADISON ARCHIVES, MADISON, WISCONSIN

Motorcycle Contingent now exist around the world and have led Pride parades in major cities on several continents.

In the 1970s, gay women (and gay men) in Wisconsin could belong to the Forker Motorcycle Club in Milwaukee. The club's members chose to call themselves the Forkers in part because the word suggests something that goes in more than one direction, like a fork in the road. Many of the group's lesbian members felt as though they had chosen the path less traveled. Donna Coleman was one of the club's cofounders. She served on the board of directors of Milwaukee's Gay People's Union from 1974 to 1978. As a lifelong Catholic, she was also involved in Milwaukee Dignity, a group offering affirmation and acceptance for LGBTQ+ Catholics. When she moved to Oxford, Wisconsin, in the late 1980s, she formed and led the Lizards of Central Wisconsin. This group of lesbians aged thirty and over met monthly to socialize.

The Forker Motorcycle Club patch below belonged to Donna Coleman, who donated it to the UW–Madison Archive in 2020. Patches like this are usually sewn onto leather jackets and display aspects of the wearer's personality or identity. The crossed motorcycles on this patch represent the Forker part of the club's name. What other elements of this patch could convey something about its owner's identity?

Forker Motorcycle Club patch, 1974–1985

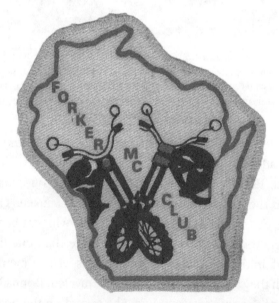

LIZARDS OF CENTRAL WISCONSIN PAPERS (DONNA COLEMAN), UNPROCESSED COLLECTION, BOX 3, FORKER MOTORCYCLE MINUTES BINDER, UNIVERSITY OF WISCONSIN–MADISON ARCHIVES, MADISON, WISCONSIN

Bi?Shy?Why?: Madison's Bisexual Group

One early group for bisexuals gave their members visibility within the larger queer community, which was often seen as including only gay men and lesbians. In 1992, bisexuals in Madison founded Bi?Shy?Why?. The organization offered support groups, attended national rallies, and published the newsletter *Bi-Lines: A Newsletter for the Bisexual Community*. The primary aim of Bi?Shy?Why? was to educate people about bisexuality. Its members believed both heterosexual and homosexual communities suffered from "biphobia."[11]

> *This source about a bisexual support group definitely speaks to me the most and is very interesting to read.*

The *Bi-Lines* article excerpt on the following page invites

Members of the Madison bisexual group Bi?Shy?Why? attended the March on Washington for Lesbian, Gay and Bi Equal Rights and Liberation in 1993. Their sign expressed their support for bisexual inclusion in the march. DAILY CARDINAL LGBTQ IMAGES, CIRCA 1960–1990, UAC68, UNIVERSITY OF WISCONSIN–MADISON ARCHIVES, MADISON, WISCONSIN

members of Bi?Shy?Why? to attend the March on Washington for Lesbian, Gay and Bi Equal Rights and Liberation in 1993. One of the largest protests in American history, this march drew an esti- mated one million attendees.[12] Though it was the third national LGBTQ+ march, it was the first national march that included bisexuals in its title.[13] The follow-up article in *Bi-Lines* reported that Bi?Shy?Why? was one of nine bisexual organizations at the event. As they marched, members chanted, "We're here, we're queer, we're in the PTA [Parent Teacher Association]," as well as "M-I-L-K, drinking milk will make you gay. Don't be cruel, don't be mean, we're just a bunch of dairy queens."[14]

Bisexual groups formed in Milwaukee and other midwestern cities in the early 1990s. The national bisexual organization BiNet also had a presence in the region at that time, publishing a BiNet Midwest newsletter out of Minneapolis. It served as a resource for bisexuals in the Midwest and promoted the inclusion of bisexuals and transgender people in LGBTQ+ communities.[15]

· · · · · · · · · · · · · ·

Excerpt from "Bi Events at the March on Washington, April 23–25, 1993" in *Bi-Lines*, February/March 1993

In 1987, over 650,000 Lesbians, Gays, their friends and relatives, con- verged on Washington, D.C. for 4 days of celebrations, protests, remem- brance, and civil disobedience. It was the largest civil rights demonstration in the history of this country, irrevocably changing the lives of every sin- gle person involved. And on April 25, 1993, we will do it again. 1993 is the first time bisexuals are included in the march.

The demands of the 1993 Lesbian Gay and Bi Equal Rights and Lib- eration March are:

1. Passage of a lesbian, gay, bisexual, and transgender (LGBT) civil rights bill and an end to discrimination by state and federal governments including the military; repeal of all sodomy laws and other laws that criminalize private sexual expression between consenting adults.

BI EVENTS AT THE MARCH ON WASHINGTON·APRIL 23-25, 1993

In 1987, over 650,000 Lesbians, Gays, their friends and relatives, converged on Washington, D.C. for 4 days of celebrations, protests, rememberance, and civil disobedience. It was the largest civil rights demonstration in the history of this country, irrevocably changing the lives of every single person involved. And on Aril 25, 1993, we will do it again. 1993 is the first time bisexuals are included in the march.

The demands of the 1993 Lesbian Gay and Bi Equal Rights and Liberation March are :

1. Passage of a lesbian, gay, bisexual, and transgender (LGBT) civil rights bill and an end to discrimination by state and federal governments including the military; repeal of all sodomy laws and other laws that criminalize private sexual expression between consenting adults.

2. A massive increase in funding for AIDS education, research, and patient care; universal access to health care including alternative therapies; and an end to sexism in medical research and health care.

3. Legislation to prevent discrimination against LGBTs in the areas of family diversity, custody, adoption and foster care, and that the definition of family includes the full diversity of all family structures.

4. Full and equal inclusion of LGBTs in the educational system, and the inclusion of LGBT studies in multicultural curricula.

5. The right to reproductive freedom and choice, to control our own bodies, and an end to sexist discrimination.

6. An end to racial and ethnic discrimination in all forms.

7. An end to discrimination and violent oppression based on actual or perceived sexual orientation/identification, race, religion, identity, sex and gender expression, disability, age, class, AIDS/HIV infection.

To get out as much information as possible about the Bi Events at the L/G/B March On Washington, we are reprinting some of the information found on the Bi Events flyer for the March.

Thousands of bisexuals and bi-friendly people will be in Washington, DC the weekend of April 23-25 for the 1993 National March On Washington For Lesbian, Gay and Bi Equal Rights and Liberation and other events.

BiNET USA Annual Meeting Friday, April 23

National Conference Celebrating Bisexuality, Saturday, April 24

Bi Celebration (post conference party) Saturday Night

March On Washington Sunday, April 25

The purpose of these events is to support and inspire one another through education, learning about Bisexual groups in other areas, and workshops. Workshops will be offered for everyone, from non-Bi's, through those just considering coming out as Bi, to long-time Bi activists.

The fees listed on the registration form are minimums, please donate more if you can. This will help us ensure that no one will be turned away because they cannot pay.

Low income is defined as students and people who make less than $15,000/year per individual or less than $20,000/year per family. A limited number of work exchange scholarships and travel scholarships are available; inquire now.

Registration acknowledgements will include directions to event sites. If you have not received confirmation by April 15, call 617-338-9595 to confirm.

All events are wheelchair accessible, including bathrooms. Free child care, fragrance-free area, rest area, and volunteer counselors are available during the conference. If you need child care or have other special needs (including ASL, large print, braille, etc.) please inform the Washington march committee in advance so that they can accommodate you. There will be no smoking in the building at the conference or the party.

Your donations will also support the sponsoring organizations, which do national and international bisexual outreach and liberation work, including conferences like this!

The National Conference Celebrating Bisexuality and the Bi Celebration are organized by:

• BiNET USA, a national bisexual political, educational and networking organization working for the equal rights and liberation of bisexuals and all oppressed people. Membership includes a newsletter. The Annual Membership Business Meeting on Friday is free to members of BiNET USA. You can join at the door or on the registration form on page 3. Address: POB 772, Washington, DC 20044-0722, USA

• East Coast Bisexual Network, Inc. (ECBN), a non-profit educational corporation which supports bisexuals and their allies around the world by publishing the International Directory of Bisexual Groups and maintaining the International Bisexual Archives, as well as supporting the creation and growth of bi groups along the east coast of the United States. Address: P.O.B. 639, Cambridge, MA 02140, USA

• Alliance of Multicultural Bisexuals (AMBi) in Washington, DC, a local

BI-LINES, FEBRUARY/MARCH 1993

2. A massive increase in funding for AIDS education, research, and patient care; universal access to health care including alternative therapies; and an end to sexism in medical research and health care.

3. Legislation to prevent discrimination against LGBTs in the areas of family diversity, custody, adoption and foster care, and that the definition of family includes the full diversity of all family structures.

4. Full and equal inclusion of LGBTs in the educational system, and the inclusion of LGBT studies in multicultural curricula.

5. The right to reproductive freedom and choice, to control our own bodies, and an end to sexist discrimination.

6. An end to racial and ethnic discrimination in all forms.

7. An end to discrimination and violent oppression based on actual or perceived sexual orientation/identification, race, religion, identity, sex and gender expression, disability, age, class, AIDS/HIV infection.

Eugene Schrang: Gender Confirmation Surgeon

Dr. Eugene Schrang was a straight ally and plastic surgeon originally from Milwaukee who performed male-to-female gender confirmation surgeries (sometimes called sex reassignment surgeries) at his clinic in Neenah, Wisconsin, from 1985 into the 2000s.[16] He performed these surgeries with compassion and a deep understanding of gender dysphoria long before most of society understood the condition. Gender dysphoria is defined as a conflict between the

Plastic surgeon Eugene Schrang, pictured here in his office in 2000, performed gender confirmation surgeries in Neenah, Wisconsin. WIKIMEDIA COMMONS; LYNN CONWAY/CREATIVE COMMONS

gender one was assigned at birth and the gender with which one identifies.[17] Dr. Schrang's description of his work included his own understanding of gender dysphoria: "Of all the afflictions human-kind must endure, Gender Dysphoria must certainly be one of the most unusual and distressing, and not because it produces great morbidity or mortality, but because the accompanying emotional conflicts can engender much unhappiness for the patient and her family with possible later problems involving her social activities and associations with colleagues at work."[18]

Dr. Schrang's sympathetic nature extended to the compre-hensive information packet he shared with surgery patients be-fore they arrived in Neenah. He hoped to put them at ease in small-town Wisconsin and in his clinic. Schrang uses the word *transsexual* in his packet, which was an acceptable term at that time for a person who does not identify with the sex they were assigned at birth. Today we use the word *transgender* instead. The packet also provided detailed descriptions of the procedures that would take place before, during, and after the surgery, so patients would know exactly what to expect. The portions of Dr. Schrang's packet that we chose to excerpt below demonstrate his desire to provide an experience that would, as he put it, "be a source of happiness for all who come to me as patients."

• • • • • • • • • • • • • •

Excerpt from Dr. Eugene Schrang's patient information packet, 1992

Dear [patient]:

This letter is intended to present you with the most pertinent information you will need regarding your transsexual surgery. It is meant to be informative about our requirements, our monetary policy and all of those things that will be necessary for you to know about your operation. Keep in mind that everyone's experiences are different and what material is presented here may not be exactly what happens to you, rather, it is intended to provide a general overview of the entire procedure.

The transgender operations are done at Theda Clark Regional Medical Center located in Neenah, Wisconsin. The town has a population of about 25,000 people and is located about 100 miles north of Milwaukee and thirty miles southwest of Green Bay on Highway 41. The city is covered by air service out of Appleton airport eight miles to the north, or Oshkosh airport eight miles to the south. The area is also serviced by Greyhound bus from Milwaukee and Green Bay. Most travel services can assist you with your travel plans.

If you have never been seen by me, you will be evaluated in my office around one o'clock in the afternoon of the day before surgery. It would therefore be advisable that you arrive either that morning or, if you wish, the day prior which would give you an opportunity to get a good night's sleep before you are seen in my office. We have an excellent hotel in town called The Valley Inn or the less expensive Twin City Motel which we suggest you consider if you are coming a day prior to your office appointment or if you intend to stay in a hotel after you have been discharged from the hospital before making a long trip home. Both The Valley Inn and Twin City Motel are located too far from the hospital to walk to after your operation. Taxi service is available, both from the hospital and from the airports. If you have already been seen by me in my office, you may proceed directly to the hospital the day before your surgery but please be there no later than 2:00 p.m. so the necessary lab work and preparations can be done before the personnel leave for home. . . .

If it is determined that you are eligible for transsexual surgery, you will be sent to Theda Clark Regional Medical Center for admission. At that time you will sign hospital consent forms, check your valuables, pay any remaining fees and get your lab work done. The hospital staff is courteous, friendly and competent and although they will be as helpful as possible, any technical questions regarding the surgery are best reserved for me. . . .

Enclosed find a map of the area and a copy of the male to female consent form which you may find helpful to read.

Hopefully the above has provided adequate information, but if not, please call our office and any one of us will gladly answer what questions you may have. It is our sincere wish that your transsexual operation will be a relatively pleasant experience—we will do everything we can to make it so.

Very sincerely yours,
Eugene A. Schrang. M.D.[19]

Be True to Yourself

Each person featured in this chapter made a choice—whether big or small—to live the life they wanted to live. They found a way to follow their chosen path and to ignore the voices that urged them in another direction for the wrong reasons. We hope these examples motivate you to be true to who you are, because self-acceptance is key!

4

Build Community

(Because There Is Strength in Numbers)

Informal networks of LGBTQ+ people have existed in Wisconsin for more than a hundred years. Letters, photographs, published works, and even guest books from establishments like Pendarvis House provide evidence of clandestine communications and gatherings occurring as early as the first decades of the 1900s. These networks provided LGBTQ+ people with a sense of community during an era when it was extremely dangerous to be out. After Stonewall, individuals who had been meeting privately or communicating remotely began to step into the public sphere. Sometimes they even created formal organizations with official headquarters and paid staff. As homosexuality was decriminalized in Wisconsin, these organizations provided many important services for the state's emerging LGBTQ+ community.[1]

Communities can be big or small, private or public, formal or informal. Throughout Wisconsin's history, LGBTQ+ folks have formed a wide range of communities in order to protect, educate, and support one another. After reading the sources in this chapter, we hope you feel inspired to seek out, join, or even form a community that's right for you!

Ted Pierce's Magic Group

Communities often develop out of common interests. Ted Pierce created an informal community with a sophisticated sense of style in the mid-1900s. Pierce was born in Chicago in 1907 and moved to Madison at the age of three. His paternal

> This story is super cool and includes a lot of different kinds of history.

grandparents had been born into slavery. He attended UW–Madison, worked as a tailor, and held the position of executive office messenger for three Wisconsin governors. He always had a unique style. While attending East High School in Madison, he earned the nickname "Our Fashion Plate," a phrase used to describe someone who dresses fashionably.

LGBTQ+ people were not openly accepted in American society during the 1940s and 1950s. Many individuals in Wisconsin were arrested for being part of "homosexual rings" at this time. Yet in Madison, Pierce created a space for gay men to gather that he described as "a magic Group centered on the 700 block of Jenifer Street."[2] The members of the group had refined tastes. They dressed stylishly, enjoyed fancy food and drink, and had cultured discussions about politics and art.[3]

As an African American gay man in the early twentieth century, Pierce cared about building a community where people like him could feel safe and free to be themselves. In addition to maintaining the community of the Jenifer Street group, he also

Ted Pierce donated his papers and photographs to the Wisconsin Historical Society. This image of him as a young man in Madison was included in the donation. WHI IMAGE ID 71483

kept up long-distance letter writing with friends. One of his longest running correspondences was with Willard Motley, an African American writer who met Pierce on Madison's Capitol Square near Pierce's tailor shop. They wrote to each other for twenty-seven years.[4] Motley's letter below was sent to Pierce in Madison from Cuernavaca, Mexico, where Motley was living and writing at the time.

Letter from Willard Motley to Ted Pierce, November 4, 1953

Apartado 248
Cuernavaca, Mexico
November 4, 1953

Dear Ted:

Just a note to say how good it was to see you and to see Madison again. The trip to the States would not have been successful and filled with perfumed memories without these two fulfilments. Yes, it was a rushed visit, and a crazy sort of Motley XXX circus than descended but I am looking forward to the time when you can come to Mexico for- say- two weeks when we can liesurely sit and talk and look at all the wonderful things here and when I can show you Mexico through my eyes and my fingertips. I know it will happen some day and I know that you will never want to go north of the border once having been here. I am looking forward to this showing of Mexico to you almost with a demon's delight.

Write to me. And remember that a bedroom awaits you here at my house in Mexico. And tonight after you read my letter look at Madison for me, at the campus, at the lake, at the beautiful things there, and remember that a part of me lives there in Madison.

As ever,

Wilbur

THEODORE PIERCE PAPERS, UNIVERSITY OF WISCONSIN–MADISON SPECIAL COLLECTIONS

Apartado 248
Cuernavaca, Mexico
November 4, 1953

Dear Ted:

Just a note to say how good it was to see you and to see Madison again. The trip to the States would not have been successful and filled with perfumed memories without these two fulfillments. Yes, it was a rushed visit, and a crazy sort of Motley circus [then] descended but I am looking forward to the time when you can come to Mexico for—say—two weeks when we can leisurely sit and talk and look at all the wonderful things here and when I can show you Mexico through my eyes and my fingertips. I know it will happen some day and I know that you will never want to go north of the border once having been here. I am looking forward to this showing of Mexico to you almost with a demon's delight.

Write to me. And remember that a bedroom awaits you here at my house in Mexico. And tonight after you read my letter look at Madison for me, at the campus, at the lake, at the beautiful things there, and remember that a part of me lives there in Madison.

As ever,
Wilmot

Lysistrata

Ted Pierce created private spaces where gay men could feel safe, but some groups founded LGBTQ+-friendly establishments that were open to the public. Some were cooperatives: organizations owned, controlled, and run by members to meet their economic, cultural, and social needs.[5] Lysistrata was a feminist cooperative in Madison. It ran a restaurant, bar, and performance space from 1977 to 1982. By providing a multipurpose space for meeting,

Bar manager Penny Caruso (seated) and bartender Meika Alberici relax behind the bar in Lysistrata in 1978. WHI IMAGE ID 67962

socializing, and entertaining, Lysistrata became a central gathering place for Madison's feminist community, which included queer women as well as feminists of all genders. The cooperative was the project of five founders: Karla Dobinski, Ruth Bleier, Andrea Mote Stelling, Catherine Rouse, and Jane Caryer. Kay Clarenbach, one of the founders of the National Organization for Women, was a silent partner in the early days of Lysistrata's operation.

The excerpt on the following page is from an early brochure produced by the Lysistrata Cooperative. Members were trying to raise funds for the restaurant and lounge. After they'd raised enough money, Lysistrata opened with a bang on New Year's Eve in 1977. It was an open, airy restaurant by day, serving lunch crowds with a select menu. At night, the bar opened and patrons danced the night away. The Madison fire and police departments both came to Lysistrata to recruit their first women officers and firefighters. For a few years, Lysistrata's softball team regularly played against a team from Taycheedah Correctional Institution for women, a collaboration that many remember fondly.

The co-op was never completely financially stable. The group wanted to provide customers with affordable prices, but it never made enough money to cover the daily operations. Around 1980, Lysistrata's founders began seeking other ways to support the co-op. They made appeals to their shareholders for more donations and even considered selling the operation. Lysistrata was set to be sold, although the paperwork had not yet been signed, when the building burned down on January 8, 1982. It was such a cold day that the firefighters couldn't use water hoses to douse the flames. Lysistrata board members were cleared of any wrongdoing, but the cause of the fire was never determined. Lysistrata's community mourned the loss of this feminist oasis.

• • • • • • • • • • • • •

Excerpt from Lysistrata fundraising brochure, ca. 1976

The Lysistrata Cooperative (Madison, Wisconsin) introduces LYSISTRATA: a feminist restaurant and lounge by women, for women and their friends. . . .

The Atmosphere

Picture Lysistrata in your mind . . . Outside, fresh painted trim, window-boxes, and awnings accent the character and charm of an older building. Flowers and hanging pots of greenery thrive in season; plantings and the exterior lighting and fixtures are attractive for all seasons.

Inside, it is a comfortable, warm and friendly place. Plants, wall hangings, arrangements of women's work in pottery, sculpture, stained glass, and graphics favor a living room feel. So does the furniture, especially in the bar and pool table area. Colors are rich, warm and soft. Carpeting and acoustical tile diminish the sound.

LYSISTRATA AND LESBIAN EPHEMERA COLLECTION, BOX 2, UNIVERSITY OF
WISCONSIN–MADISON ARCHIVES, MADISON, WISCONSIN

In the dining room, booths and tables for two and for four offer quiet places for women to celebrate events or conduct their business, away from the ordinary frenzy.

The big round table in the dining room will be for women who come in with friends but want to meet others, for those who know they can always find good company here for dinner, for those who think good conversation goes with good food. It is there for the same reason Lysistrata is: to provide a place where women of differing ages, views and life experiences can gather, get to know each other, discuss issues of mutual interest, give each other support.

Special catered luncheons for meetings of women's groups, a separate area capable of multiple use (entertainment, presentations, dancing), a system for collecting and displaying information on jobs, programs, problems of special concern to women—all these we see there as well.

Wisconsin Womyn's Land Cooperative

Another Wisconsin cooperative founded in the 1970s wanted to provide a more exclusive space for a specific segment of the LGBTQ+ community. In the 1970s and early 1980s, feminist separatism was a national movement that encouraged women to separate from men to achieve freedom and independence. Thousands of women across the country established land cooperatives where they moved to live among only women.[6] One of those groups was the Womyn's Land Cooperative in rural Norwalk, Wisconsin.

Founded in 1977, the lesbian co-op included an eighty-acre parcel of land where some individuals worked and lived year-round and others visited. In 1980, the co-op had 250 members. One of the group's fundamental rules was that "there would be no intrusions by men, for none were welcome on the land."[7] The group used *womyn*, an alternate spelling of *women*, to avoid including the suffix *men*, which they thought contributed to the idea that women were inferior to men. This spelling was popular during the second-wave feminist movement of the era.

At the time of this book's publication, the Womyn's Land Cooperative still exists, but its policies have changed. People may join the co-op through invitation only.[8] In recent decades, many womyn-only gatherings and spaces have been confronted with the complications of their "no men allowed" stance. Some groups have refused to include anyone who was assigned male at birth, regardless of that person's gender identity. The LGBTQ+ community largely opposes this exclusion of transgender people. As a result, many feminist and lesbian separatist organizations have disbanded, including the Michigan Womyn's Music Festival in 2015.[9]

The 2010–2011 brochure on the following page provides information about Daughters Of the Earth campground, managed by the Womyn's Land Cooperative. After reading this section and

This sketch of the Daughters Of the Earth farm from a 1978 Womyn's Land Cooperative brochure includes the moon, a symbol often associated with women. ARCHIVES DEPARTMENT, UNIVERSITY OF WISCONSIN–MILWAUKEE LIBRARIES

the previous one, do you think the Womyn's Land Cooperative and the Lysistrata Cooperative had more similarities or differences between them? If you were a lesbian in the late 1970s, would one of these feminist communities appeal to you more than the other?

• • • • • • • • • • • •

Excerpt from Daughters Of the Earth Campground for Womyn brochure, 2010–2011

HERSTORY:

In 1977, a group of womyn from Wisconsin and Minnesota decided they wanted a space of their own in the country to be themselves. They formed Wisconsin Womyn's Land Co-op and went looking for that space.

They soon found an 80 acre parcel of land for sale that suited their needs. They raised the down payment, and Daughters Of the Earth (DOE) was born.

In the early years, the co-op developed into a hybrid of consumer and worker aspects. There have been many womyn who lived here on

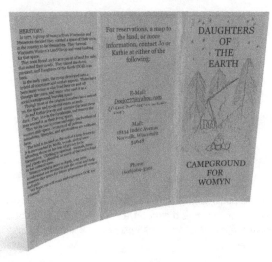

SPECIAL COLLECTIONS, UNIVERSITY OF WISCONSIN–MILWAUKEE LIBRARIES

and off through the years, and many who used it as a social/campground/ learning space.

Though most of the original founders have moved on, the space and co-op still exists as such.

Jo and Kathie live on and caretake the land these days. They live in the farmhouse, and reserve the area around it as their living space.

They invite you to come and enjoy the freedom of womyn only space. Womyn of all politics, sexualities, lifestyles, and spiritualities are welcome here.

The land is located on the end of a long driveway. It is surrounded by bluffs, woods, and ravines, affording those on her lots of privacy to be themselves. Clothing is optional. Animals, trees, and plants are plentiful, as much of the land is kept in her natural state.

Womyn wishing more in depth, long term involvement are invited to join the co-op and help preserve this space for future generations of womyn and girls.

We hope you will come and experience DOE for yourself.

Gay Travel Guides

LGBTQ+ individuals also created networks to communicate about safe and unsafe public spaces. Before Stonewall, very few establishments publicly advertised themselves as gay bars or gay friendly businesses. However, sometimes by design and sometimes by chance, many bars, clubs, and restaurants were popular meeting spots for LGBTQ+ folks. Bars often provided the only pre-Stonewall centers for socializing among sexual minority people, many of whom were closeted.

In the mid-1960s, LGBTQ+ community members began to publish "gay travel guides." The guides listed

This early gay travel guide from 1964 listed LGBTQ+ friendly establishments in Fond du Luc, Green Bay, Madison, Milwaukee, and Oshkosh. CANADIAN LESBIAN AND GAY ARCHIVES VIA GALE PRIMARY SOURCES ARCHIVES OF SEXUALITY AND GENDER

and described establishments (primarily bars) where LGBTQ+ folks gathered. Some guides used symbols and codes to indicate the times or days of the week when gay people would be welcomed or the crowds one might expect to see at certain bars.[10] By using these guides, readers could seek out like-minded people while avoiding spots that might be unfriendly or dangerous. Can you think of any guides or codes that are used among LGBTQ+ people today?

Places of Interest was an international guide that described itself as "designed specifically for the gay traveler in the USA and Canada."[11] It provided maps and listings about gay life in cities across both countries. Its symbols and abbreviations described establishments in detail. The excerpts on the following pages show the guide's symbols and listings for Green Bay, Hurley, and La Crosse in 1986.

• • • • • • • • • • • • • •
• • • • • • • • • • • • •

Excerpts from *Places of Interest* 1986

	men hommes hombres Manner mannen		**women** femmes mujeres Frauen vrouwen	
	hustlers commerciaux prostitucion masculina Stricher		**nudity permitted** nudisme permis se permite desnudo Nacktheit erlaubt naaktheid veroorloofd	

GAY SYMBOLS — men: hommes, hombres, Manner, mannen; hustlers: commerciaux, prostitucion masculina, Stricher; leather: cuir, cuero, Leder, leer; oriental: orientaux, orientales, Asiaten, oosters; cocktails: cocteles, Bar, Coctailbar, sterke dranken; no alcohol: pas d'alcool, Getranke verboten, geen dranken; dancing: danse, lugar bailable, Tanzen, dansen; toilet: crotte, sucio, Toilette; very young: tres jeunes, muy jovenes, fur sehr Junge, erg jong; swimming pool: piscine, piscina, Schwimmbecken, zwembad; country & western: tipo oeste, Contry & Western.

women: femmes, mujeres, Frauen, vrouwen; nudity permitted; levi: costumes levi-western, vaqueros, Westernkneipe, spijkerbroek; latin: latins, latinos, mexikanisch, latijns; go go: bailarines, go go, dansers; beer & wine: biere et vin, cerveza y vino, nur Bier und Wein, Alleen bier en wijn; food: collation, comida, Imbiss zu haben, eten; fantasy: phantasme, fantasias, Phantasie, fantasie; older: plus agees, personas mayores, fur Altere, oudere personen; straight/not gay: plutot heterosexuelle, heterosexual, hetero.

men and women: hommes-femmes, hombres y mujeres, Manner und Frauen, mannen en vrouwen; cruisy: dragueurs, gut zum Abschleppen; back room: cuarto oscuro, Dunkelraum, donkere achterkamer; black & white: noirs et blancs, negros y blancos, Schwarze/Weisse, zwart en blank; neighborhood: bar du quartier, bar de vecinidad, Nachbarschaft umgevung, buurt kroeg; bring your own liquor: apporter boissons, traer su propria bebida, alkoholische Getranke durfen mitgebracht werden; female impressionist: spectacles travestis, espectaculos travestis, Travetichow, vrouwen verpersoon lijkings show; live entertainment: spectacles, espectaculos, live Unterhaltung, "live" vermaak; uniforms: costumes militaires, uniformes militaires, Uniformen, uniformen; business/professionals: hommes/femmes d'affairs, profesionales, geschaftlich, beruflich, zakenlui/vakmensen.

PLACES OF INTEREST 1986

Green Bay (414)

Bars/Dance Bars

1. LOFT, 2328 University Ave nr
   Peters, 468-9968, dance bar, men
   welcome

2. MY WORLD, 409 S Washington
   nr Crooks, 432-3917, name may
   change

3. NAPALES LOUNGE, 515 S Broadway nr Clinton, 432-9646,

4. TRIX'S ALL-STAR JOYNT, 121 S
   Washington St nr Doty, 435-4064,
   dance bar

5. WHO'S, 720 Bodart Way nr
   Jackson (rear), 435-5476,
   Video/dance bar, Su Buffet

Restaurants

MARTHA'S, 519 S Broadway
24hrs, pop aft hrs

Services (All)

AA (GAY/LESB), Tu 8, Fri 7, at Napales
Lounge
DIGNITY, 739-8030, Appleton/Green Bay
WOMEN'S SERVICE CTR, 433-6667, ans
service can connect you

Erotica

BOOKS & THINGS, 753 Lombardi at Gross,
499-5797

WISCONSIN

PARADISE, 1122 Main St nr Webster,
432-9498, 24hrs

Hurley (715)

Accommodations

LAMBDA HOUSE, near Ironwood,
WI, (Hwy 2 & 51), 561-3120,
bed/breakfast, near skiing, write: PO
BOX 20, Pence, 54553

LaCrosse (608)

Bars/Dance Bars

TATOO'S II, 1542 Rose St nr
Gillett, 782-9529/6194, dance bar

Services (All)

GAY MEN'S GROUP (LAGA), 782-0963, activities, raps
WOMEN'S GROUP, monthly events,
783-0069

Madison (608)

Information Lines

ALL GAYS CRISIS LINE, 255-4297, 9-6 7dys

Bars/Dance Bars

1. BACK EAST, 508 E Wilson St nr
   Franklin, 256-7104, dance bar

Copyright © 1985 by Ferrari Publications. This map may not be reproduced wholly or in
part without written permission from the publishers

155

PLACES OF INTEREST 1986

The Fire Ball Drag Show

While change sometimes feels slow, events like the Fire Ball at UW–Eau Claire (UWEC) show that progress is being made in communities across Wisconsin. A hearing was held by the Governor's Council on Lesbian and Gay Issues in Eau Claire in the 1980s. The LGBTQ+ locals talked about the issues they faced, from violence to a lack of emotional and financial support. Most agreed that Eau Claire County was not a welcoming place for the LGBTQ+ community.[12] However, UWEC students led the charge to change Eau Claire's reputation in the following decades.

In the early 1980s, a gay and lesbian organization (which later expanded to included bisexuals) was founded on the UWEC campus. An LGBTQ+ paper called *New Beginnings* covered gay news in Eau Claire and La Crosse between 1987 and 1991. It included

The theme of UW–Eau Claire's 2017 Fire Ball, pictured here, was PULSE. It was named in honor and remembrance of the 2016 mass shooting at a gay nightclub called Pulse in Orlando, Florida. The Fire Ball's organizers wanted to demonstrate that hate cannot stop pride. THE FIRE BALL, UNIVERSITY OF WISCONSIN-EAU CLAIRE

a regular column by an Eau Claire drag performer.[13] And the campus has continued to become more LGBTQ+ friendly. The Eau Queer Film Festival began in 2010 and the Fire Ball (sometimes spelled Fireball) held its first drag show in 2011. In 2017, UWEC was ranked third in the nation on a list of the "50 Best Colleges for LGBTQ Students" by College Choice.[14]

The Fire Ball was initially organized to raise money for the UWEC Gender and Sexuality Resource Center. It became an elaborate two-night drag show that brings top-notch performers to the university. For many attendees, the Fire Ball is a safe space to learn about sexuality in a celebratory way. As the performer Katya mentions in the article below, the Fire Ball is proof that small cities and rural areas throughout the country are increasingly creating welcoming and supportive environments for LGBTQ+ people.

• • • • • • • • • • • •

Excerpt from "Eau Claire's Fireball Drag Show is Back in Town," in *BluGold Media*, February 2016

In the words of legendary drag superstar RuPaul, "We're all born naked, and the rest is drag."

And that is exactly the approach Fireball 2016 has taken. With the theme "Stripped," the drag show is promising a night of eleganza with an edge.

University of Wisconsin–Eau Claire's Women's and LGBTQ Resource Center coordinator, Christopher Jorgenson, forefronts Fireball's direction. Jorgenson said he tries to come up with a distinctive theme each year to ensure innovation.

"Last year our theme was Pretty Dirty. It was dark—it was grungy, so I wanted to do the exact opposite," Jorgenson said.

While aesthetically, the white décor compliments the idea of

"Stripped," Jorgenson suggests that there is also an underlying meaning behind the theme.

"Given the budget situation in the state of Wisconsin, I think [this theme] has some meta," Jorgenson said. "Even though some seek to defund higher education, we can still do incredible and important programming."

Jorgenson did not hesitate to ensure the Fireball is prepared for success, booking two headliners from RuPaul's Drag Race Season 7 for this weekend. Drag Queen Kennedy Davenport will be headlining Friday night, and fan-favorite Katya leads Saturday's show. . . .

Jorgenson said once Friday's headliner was chosen, picking Katya for Saturday came naturally.

"She is such a powerful blend of being a dynamic performer, but also being really funny—irreverently funny," Jorgenson said. "I think the Fireball is in a really good position to challenge the community, and I thought Katya will fit in really well with this idea."

Katya describes herself as a "multifaceted charismatic woman of grace, dignity and sexual ambiguity and promiscuity." . . .

When asked if she knew much about Eau Claire, Katya gave a light-hearted laugh and admitted that she had never heard of it before.

"I generally just kind of go where my manager tells me to. The thing is, it's funny with gigs like this because often I look at my calendar and see that there is a city listed like Eau Claire, and say, okay interesting, Wisconsin," Katya said. "But these gigs are often the best experiences for me, even more so than your typical New York, San Francisco, or LA gigs." . . .

She said performing through drag has the impact to inspire people and make a difference in terms of activism and pride.

"Look, we are not curing cancer here," she said with a laugh, "but we are getting people excited and motivated and interested in being themselves."

Two Teenagers in Twenty

In this chapter, we've covered different types of communities formed by and for LGBTQ+ adults, but we have not yet heard directly from LGBTQ+ teenagers. In the personal essay on the following

> *I love this story because I think it really speaks to the teenage experience.*

page, eighteen-year-old Jennifer Hanrahan describes her three-year journey from being a bisexual who was not out and had no gay friends to being a proud and active member of Milwaukee's LGBTQ+ community.

Hanrahan's essay is just one of many written by American teenagers in the 1994 book *Two Teenagers in Twenty*, the follow up to the 1983 book *One Teenager in Ten*. Both volumes were collected and edited by Ann Heron. "One in ten" and "two in twenty" are references to the rumored number of LGBTQ+ people in the general population. The contested statistic says that about 10 percent of people identify as LGBTQ+, whether or not they are out.[15] The books' titles, as well as the essays inside, were meant to provide young LGBTQ+ readers with a sense of belonging.

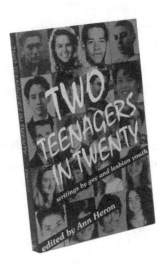

One review of *One Teenager in Ten* demonstrates how much these books meant to some young readers: "I read this as a teenager in the 80s. I lived in a rural area [and] didn't knowingly have any contact with other GLBT people. This book

Two Teenagers in Twenty, edited by Ann Heron, published essays by gay and lesbian youth from across the nation in 1994.
ALYSON PUBLICATIONS

helped me feel connected. It also made clear to me [that] other people's problems with homosexuality [are] just that . . . THEIR PROBLEM[S]."[16] In an age before the internet, *One Teenager in Ten* and *Two Teenagers in Twenty* provided important examples of LGBTQ+ teenagers figuring out how to be themselves and find community. Do you think aspects of Hanrahan's story still ring true for today's LGBTQ+ teens? What has changed since 1994?

• • • • • • • • • • • • •

Excerpt from "Jennifer Hanrahan, 18: Milwaukee, Wisconsin" in *Two Teenagers in Twenty*, 1994

Most of the time, I call myself bisexual, but I dislike labels. They tend to box you in. My sexuality shifts from day to day. Some days I feel very gay; I'm attracted only to women. Other days I feel very straight. Some days I'm just plain confused! Overall, I'd say I'm more attracted to women than to men, at least physically.

I realized I wasn't straight about three years ago, when I found myself hopelessly infatuated with a straight girlfriend. I tried to ignore it, but I couldn't stop thinking about her. Every time I thought I might be gay, I became very scared. I didn't know any gay people (at least, I thought I didn't), and I was worried about what people would think of me.

I avoided the issue for another year. I didn't see my friend very much during that time, so it was easy to ignore the fact that I might be gay. But then I fell in love with one of my teachers—a married woman. This time I couldn't deny what I felt. I thought I must be bisexual. I certainly couldn't be straight. It scared me to death. I was obsessed with keeping it a secret. I even wrote notes in my diary in code so that no one would suspect I was one of "those people." . . .

I still didn't know any openly gay people, so I decided to find some. I saw an ad in the local weekly paper for an ACT UP (AIDS Coalition to

Unleash Power) meeting at a local church. I had heard of ACT UP in the national news, and figured there would be gay people there. I was right. Just about everyone at the meeting was gay. I met Patrick there, and he became a good friend. I made many connections through the people that I met that night. I learned about Gay Youth Milwaukee, Queer Nation, and the Gay Lesbian Bisexual Community at the University of Wisconsin (GLBC). Over the next few months, I met many more gay people. I've learned that gays and lesbians are everywhere. It's just that many times, they're invisible. It takes searching to bring them out of the woodwork....

I'm still involved with ACT UP and GLBC. I have a wide network of friends who listen when I have problems with my parents or get sick of the straight world. Sometimes I get tired of being bisexual. I get sick of people calling us names, putting us down, saying we spread AIDS, and so on. I'm sick of having to lie to my grandparents: they would disown me if they found out. I cry when I think of my friends Jay and Chris, who have AIDS. Whenever I hear of someone getting fired, evicted, beat up, or killed because they are gay, I am disgusted and angry. Sometimes I just wish I was straight. I wish I was "normal" like everyone else.

But being gay and being involved in the gay community has made me a stronger person. I am not ashamed of what I am. I feel pride when I see one of "my people" in Congress; honor when I see them battling discrimination in the military; respect when my friends risk arrest to fight AIDS; and dignity when I speak to a high school group and tell them that we are people, just like them.

I want to do something for the gay community, especially gay and lesbian youth. We carry the heaviest burden. We are already dealing with everything that all teenagers have to go through. Then, on top of that, we have to deal with society's taboos against our sexuality, rejection from family and friends, gay-bashers, and AIDS. I'm surprised any of us makes it.

But I believe someday things will be better for us. They're getting better all the time. Meanwhile, we have to stay strong individually and as a community. To any young gays or bisexuals reading this: Don't listen

ALYSON PUBLICATIONS

to the lies that straight society spreads or the names they call us. To borrow an old civil rights slogan, "Gay Is Okay!" Don't let anyone else tell you different. Try to find the gay community in your area. Everything is easier with someone by your side who knows how you feel. I know what a lonely feeling growing up gay can be. But believe me, *you are not alone.*

Build Community

LGBTQ+ Wisconsinites have been forming communities for more than a hundred years, even when it was dangerous, in order to feel safe, accepted, and loved. If you feel alone, know there are other people like you out there! Communities come in all shapes and sizes. We hope the examples in this chapter expand your understanding of what a community can be. We encourage you to find or build a community that works for you, because there is strength in numbers.

5

Get Active

(Because Change Is Always Possible)

So far, this book has explored many forms of activism, from
seeking an education and telling your story to expressing your
identity and building a community. But people also create change
by actively supporting or opposing a political issue. How have people engaged in political action to make change in Wisconsin? Some
people file lawsuits and work through the justice system. Occasionally, a court's decision on one case will affect people across the
state, and even throughout the nation. People can work through
the legislative system by voicing their opinions to political officials. Some even run for elected office themselves. Others draw
attention to important issues by putting up posters, speaking at
public events, and participating in demonstrations. Many people
take action to change systems that affect them personally, but
some take action on behalf of others or for society as a whole. It
can take a long time, but change is always possible thanks to people who decide to take a stand.

This chapter provides examples of actions that effected real
change in Wisconsin's LGBTQ+ community. They add up to just a
tiny sliver of what activism can look like. We hope they open your
eyes to some of the many ways that you can make a change in the
world.

Jamie Nabozny's Court Case

Some people effect change by seeking justice through the judicial branch of our government. This branch interprets the meaning of the Constitution. The Constitution and its Bill of Rights were ratified in 1791. While the documents promised "the blessings of liberty" to the "people of the United States," many groups were

> This source about students in a school getting discriminated against speaks to me most because in my school this topic is not discussed in history classes (even AP history).

left out of those promises.[1] American Indians, African Americans, and women of all races were not explicitly protected in the original Constitution or the Bill of Rights. Over the following centuries, another seventeen amendments have been added to provide rights and protections to more Americans.

We learn in school that the US government is divided into three branches: executive, legislative, and judicial. The legislative branch (Congress) passes laws, which can include some protections. The executive branch (the president) can issue executive orders to extend protections. And the judicial branch (judges in courts) has the job of interpreting those laws and orders in the cases brought to courts. Judicial interpretations of laws can result in important changes to American life. Many protections for LGBTQ+ people have come out of courtrooms. One of these cases was that of a young man in Ashland, Wisconsin, who brought a lawsuit against his school district for allowing harassment.

Jamie Nabozny grew up Ashland and came out as gay at age thirteen.[2] Starting in 1988, when he was in seventh grade, and continuing into high school, he was bullied about his sexual orientation. The high school principal, Mary Podlesny, sided with the bullies. She dismissed their behavior by saying "boys will be boys."[3] The harassment continued until 1992 when Nabozny ran away to

Minneapolis. He eventually got his high school diploma and was admitted to the University of Minnesota.[4]

In 1995, Nabozny filed a lawsuit against his former school district and several school officials for failing to protect his Fourteenth Amendment rights. His lawyers argued that Nabozny was being discriminated against because he belonged to a minority group as a gay teen. The lawsuit traveled through the court system, and Nabozny was ultimately paid $900,000 in damages. Three school district administrators were ordered to pay the amount, and the school district was found not guilty.[5] An excerpt from the judge's final decision in the case appears on the following pages.

Nabozny's case helped to give young people across the nation more protections under the law. The lawsuit helped clarify the role of schools in bullying motivated by gender and sexual orientation. A federal law called Title IX, which protects people from sex-based discrimination in education programs and government-funded activities, was also amended. The change required all US schools to provide a harassment-free environment to gay and lesbian students. Thanks in part to Jamie Nabozny's actions, kids who are bullied in schools today can feel protected under the law and less alone.[6] As an adult, Nabozny made a career as a safe-school advocate, married, and raised a family.[7]

Bullied, a short documentary released in 2010, shares the story of Jamie Nabozny's historic lawsuit against the Ashland school district. SOUTHERN POVERTY LAW CENTER

• • • • • • • • • • • • •

Excerpt from the judge's decision in *Nabozny v. Podlesny*, US Court of Appeals, 1996

Jamie Nabozny was a student in the Ashland Public School District (hereinafter "the District") in Ashland, Wisconsin throughout his middle school and high school years. During that time, Nabozny was continually harassed and physically abused by fellow students because he is homosexual. Both in middle school and high school Nabozny reported the harassment to school administrators. Nabozny asked the school officials to protect him and to punish his assailants. Despite the fact that the school administrators had a policy of investigating and punishing student-on-student battery and sexual harassment, they allegedly turned a deaf ear to Nabozny's requests. Indeed, there is evidence to suggest that some of the administrators themselves mocked Nabozny's predicament. Nabozny eventually filed suit against several school officials and the District pursuant to 42 U.S.C. § 1983 alleging, among other things, that the defendants: 1) violated his Fourteenth Amendment right to equal protection by discriminating against him based on his gender; 2) violated his Fourteenth Amendment right to equal protection by discriminating against him based on his sexual orientation; 3) violated his Fourteenth Amendment right to due process by exacerbating the risk that he would be harmed by fellow students; and 4) violated his Fourteenth Amendment right to due process by encouraging an environment in which he would be harmed. The defendants filed a motion for summary judgment, which the district court granted. Nabozny appeals the district court's decision. Because we agree with the district court only in part, we affirm in part, reverse in part, and remand....

Conclusion.

We conclude that, based on the record as a whole, a reasonable fact-finder could find that the District and defendants Podlesny, Davis, and Blauert violated Nabozny's Fourteenth Amendment right to equal protection by discriminating against him based on his gender or sexual orientation. Further, the law establishing the defendants' liability was sufficiently clear to inform the defendants at the time that their conduct was unconstitutional. Nabozny's equal protection claims against the District, Podlesny, Davis, and Blauert are reinstated in toto. We further conclude that Nabozny has failed to produce sufficient evidence to permit a reasonable fact-finder to find that the defendants violated Nabozny's Fourteenth Amendment right to due process either by enhancing his risk of harm or by encouraging a climate to flourish in which he suffered harm. Our disposition of Nabozny's due process claims renders the district court's award of qualified immunity as to those claims moot. The decision of the district court is

AFFIRMED IN PART, REVERSED IN PART, AND REMANDED.

• • • • • • • • • • • • • •

Judy Greenspan's School Board Run

Decades prior to Jamie Nabozny's case, one LGBTQ+ woman ran for a seat on her local school board (a representative form of school government) as a way to fight back against discrimination. In 1972, at the age of twenty, Judy Greenspan was an out lesbian and a student at UW–Madison. A Madison East High School teacher invited Greenspan and other members of the Madison Gay Liberation Front to speak at an upcoming workshop on sexual identity and orientation. The school's principal quickly stopped the plans and created a policy with other principals to ban all gay and lesbian speakers in Madison high schools. The school board approved the policy on June 7, 1972.[8] Can you think of any subjects that might create a controversy like this when talked about in high schools today?

Greenspan decided to get politically active and run for a seat on the school board for the 1973 election. She is believed to have been the first out lesbian in the United States to run for elected office.[9] Ironically, Greenspan's candidacy in the school board election created a new opportunity for her to speak to high school students (though not in classrooms). The *Capital Times* noted, "As a lesbian she is not permitted to enter public schools without the principal's permission, but as a candidate she has already been invited to speak at Memorial High [at a school board meeting]."[10] Greenspan ran a low-budget campaign, but her messages were clear, as you can see in her campaign poster on the following page. She believed in her ideas and in mobilizing her community to support her. When interviewed by a Madison feminist newspaper, she noted, "Running openly as a lesbian and a feminist is going to be a hard job. I hope my sisters will actively participate in the campaign."[11] Greenspan advocated for women's rights. She brought a lesbian perspective into conversations about conditions for gay and lesbian teachers and students, students' education about gay issues, and other school matters.

On March 6, 1973, Greenspan lost the primary election, but she did win 6,000 votes.[12] Her historic run eventually led to more visibility and victories for other openly gay politicians from Wisconsin, such as Tammy Baldwin (the nation's first out gay person elected to the US Senate) and Mark Pocan (an out gay man elected to the US House of Representatives). Greenspan later moved to Berkeley, California, where she still resides with her partner and engages in activism.[13]

• • • • • • • • • • • • • •

Judy Greenspan for School Board campaign poster, 1973

WHI IMAGE ID 59050

• • • • • • • • • • • • •

Wisconsin Goes to Washington

Running for elected office is one way to become involved in the political process. Another way everyday citizens can influence policy is by participating in demonstrations. Marches, rallies, parades, and walks have long been ways to get active and show support for or against causes. The history of activism in the United States includes many demonstrations as forms of peaceful protest. In the early 1900s, women took to the streets to demand the right to vote. In the 1960s, participants in the civil rights movement pushed for racial justice in many iconic marches. The first Pride celebration took place around the one-year anniversary of the Stonewall uprising. Pride parades, in various forms, have been held near this date every year since. Gathering and marching in large crowds are great ways to visually demonstrate the feelings people have for a particular cause.

A delegation from Madison represented Wisconsin in the 1979 March on Washington for Lesbian and Gay Rights. DAILY CARDINAL LGBTQ IMAGES, CIRCA 1960–1990, UAC68, UNIVERSITY OF WISCONSIN–MADISON ARCHIVES, MADISON, WISCONSIN

In 1979, Wisconsin activists marched in the first March on Washington for Lesbian and Gay Rights. In 1987, lesbian and gay Dane County supervisors Tammy Baldwin, Dick Wagner, and Kathleen Nichols represented Wisconsin at the Second National March on Washington for Lesbian and Gay Rights. Along with other marchers from Wisconsin, they chanted, "WIS-CON-SIN, the Gay Rights State."[14] Wisconsin was called the Gay Rights State because of its statewide ban on discrimination against homosexuals, a law that had passed in 1982. An article in the *Wisconsin Light* reported, "Throughout the March route, many of the thousands lining the street joined in the chant as gays and lesbians from throughout America saluted our state and expressed their appreciation for the hope we have given them."[15]

Washington DC APRIL 25, 1993

DON'T MISS THIS ONE!

This drawing, which appeared in the February/March 1993 issue of *Bi-Lines*, encouraged Bi?Shy?Why? members to attend the March on Washington for Lesbian, Gay and Bi Equal Rights and Liberation. It was the third national LGBTQ+ march (see page 68 for more information on this march). *BI-LINES*, FEBRUARY/MARCH 1993

In the photograph on the following page, Baldwin, Wagner, and Nichols stand on Langdon Street in Madison with UW–Madison's Memorial Library in the background, holding the banner they carried in the national march in Washington, DC. If you were attending or watching this march in Washington in 1987, how might you have reacted to this banner?

• • • • • • • • • • • • •

Photograph of Wisconsin's out elected officials, 1987

COURTESY OF DICK WAGNER

• • • • • • • • • • • • •

Lloyd Barbee's Gay Rights Advocacy

Wisconsin earned its nickname as the Gay Rights State because of the actions of many advocates, including some allies, who significantly contributed to the state's LGBTQ+ movement. Governor Tony Earl (see page 61 for more information on Earl) was one advocate who used his platform to create real change in Wisconsin. He commissioned a Governor's Council on Lesbian and Gay Issues

In this 1975 picture, Wisconsin governor Patrick Lucey (sitting) ratifies the Equal Rights Amendment as Lloyd Barbee (far left), a supporter, looks on. The amendment was designed to guarantee equal rights to all American citizens, regardless of their sex. At the time of this book's publication, it still has not been ratified by enough states to pass into law. WHI IMAGE ID 97430

and signed a bill that decriminalized homosexual acts in Wisconsin in 1983, among other actions. Lloyd Barbee was another early advocate who laid the foundation for these later legislative successes in Wisconsin.

Lloyd Barbee is best known for his work in the Black communities of Wisconsin, but he was also a great champion of the state's LGBTQ+ citizens. Born in Tennessee, Barbee joined the NAACP (the National Association for the Advancement of Colored People) at the age of twelve. He earned a law degree at UW–Madison and worked for the state before setting up a law practice in Milwaukee. He then ran for state representative of the Sixth District. From 1964 until 1977, he was the only African American in the Wisconsin State Legislature. As a representative, Barbee worked tirelessly against segregation and helped lead the effort to integrate the racially segregated Milwaukee Public Schools. Throughout his entire life he worked for social justice and change.[16]

Many Wisconsinites know that Barbee sponsored bills on fair housing, civil rights, and multicultural history education. Fewer know that he was fundamental in introducing bills to support LGBTQ+ rights. In 1967, he was the first Wisconsin lawmaker to introduce a bill to decriminalize homosexuality. And in 1971, he introduced a bill to protect gay and lesbian workers from job discrimination, as well as one of the first bills in the nation to legalize same-sex marriage.[17] His bills did not receive enough support to pass during those decades. However, they had the important effect of educating Wisconsin lawmakers and the general public about LGBTQ+ issues.

The excerpt below is from Barbee's speech at UW–Oshkosh in 1973. He spoke out against laws that penalized people for victimless crimes, including the Wisconsin laws that criminalized homosexual acts. Throughout his political life, Barbee fought for an inclusive world that respected the rights of all people: Black people, American Indians, non-English speakers, women, prisoners, and LGBTQ+ individuals.[18]

• • • • • • • • • • • • • •

Excerpt from "Victimless Crimes," a speech by Lloyd Barbee at UW–Oshkosh, December 2, 1973

Other areas of criminal law that need reforming are the "sex statutes." It's time the government is taken out of the bedroom. We should remove all state curbs on sexual activities between consenting parties, married or otherwise. This would keep sexual matters where they should be, in the private realm of personal choice between individuals.

Specifically, we should remove the criminal penalties for homosexuals, adultery, fornication, cohabitation, and possession of "indecent materials" when such actions do not involve minors under 14.

It makes little sense for governments to condone and support the necessity of war while at the same time, make illegal various acts of love. With the sex statutes as they are written today in this state, we've probably got a populace of criminals. And this is absurd.

●●●●●●●●●●●●●●●

The HIV/AIDS Epidemic

Almost no other event in LGBTQ+ history has motivated more individuals to take action than the HIV/AIDS epidemic of the 1980s and 1990s. This public health crisis resulted in hundreds of thousands of deaths in the United States and many

> *I like this source because I am part of the LGBTQ+ community, and before, I did not know about AIDS.*

more around the world. The LGBTQ+ community was devastated by this infectious disease and blamed for it, especially in the early years of the epidemic when many believed that only gay people and drug users were affected.

Some LGBTQ+ people with HIV/AIDS were outed without their permission when hospitals called their families and revealed their diagnoses. Some patients' families were not supportive of their sexual orientation and did not allow patients' partners and friends to visit them in the hospital while they were dying. These tragic experiences were recalled in legal battles decades later when gay people fought to gain marriage rights. Now that two people can be considered legal spouses regardless of their gender, they cannot be barred from visiting one another in hospital rooms.

The AIDS epidemic encouraged LGBTQ+ people and their loved ones to become active in many ways. Some worked to memorialize those who had died, to ensure that the tragedy of the global epidemic would not be lost to history. In 1987, a group of strangers in San Francisco started the NAMES Project AIDS

A couple visits the AIDS Memorial Quilt in the UW–Madison field house in 1991. Those viewing the quilt would often look for squares commemorating people they knew. DAILY CARDINAL LGBTQ IMAGES, CIRCA 1960–1990, UAC68, UNIVERSITY OF WISCONSIN–MADISON ARCHIVES, MADISON, WISCONSIN

Memorial Quilt. The quilt was a traveling memorial to those who had lost their lives to AIDS-related illnesses. Each square of the quilt was designed and created by friends, partners, and families to commemorate their loved ones. The quilt is made up of more than 48,000 squares.[19] If displayed in whole, it would be roughly the size of Sheboygan in 2020. Portions of the quilt have been displayed in Madison and Milwaukee.[20]

Since the 1980s, members of the LGBTQ+ community impacted by HIV/AIDS have supported each other at many community events, such as this candlelight vigil for those lost to AIDS. DAILY CARDINAL LGBTQ IMAGES, CIRCA 1960–1990, UAC68, UNIVERSITY OF WISCONSIN–MADISON ARCHIVES, MADISON, WISCONSIN

Compared to many other states, Wisconsin responded quickly and early to the AIDS crisis. The Governor's Council on Gay and Lesbian Issues held meetings to address the crisis as early as June 1983, months before a Wisconsin newspaper reported the state's first AIDS-related death.[21] The "Statement Concerning AIDS" below demonstrates the compassionate care for patients that was recommended in November 1983 by the Wisconsin Medical Society. Because of these and other educational efforts made by Wisconsinites—from local health clinics to the state's AIDS task force to activist organizations like ACT-UP (the AIDS Coalition to Unleash Power)—a smaller percentage of the population in Wisconsin died from AIDS than in many other states.

From the beginning of the epidemic to 2020, globally, 32 million people have died of HIV/AIDS.[22] The virus is not gone, but it has become better managed in many areas due to active educational outreach about transmission, treatment, and methods of prevention. Learning more about HIV/AIDS may inspire you to ensure the stories from the epidemic are not forgotten.

• • • • • • • • • • • • • •

Excerpt from "Statement Concerning AIDS" from the State Medical Society of Wisconsin, September 17, 1983

The first cases of what is now identified as acquired immune deficiency syndrome (AIDS) were reported two years ago. More than 2,000 cases have been reported nationwide, with perhaps as many as 20 confirmed or suspected cases thus far in Wisconsin. The death rate among AIDS cases is very high.

The cause of AIDS is as yet unknown, as is effective treatment. However, the clinical characteristics of the syndrome have been quite well defined, the scientific and clinical studies are growing rapidly, and to some extent the growing body of knowledge is easing some of the disturbing and seldom documented stories of lack of care available to patients who have or suspect they have AIDS.

The Board of Directors of the State Medical Society considers it important at this stage of the understanding about AIDS to make these observations:

- An open nonjudgmental attitude is basic to all good patient care. The sick individual (heterosexual or homosexual) deserves the best care the profession has to offer for all physical or mental conditions.

Statement concerning AIDS

Adopted by the Board of Directors of the State Medical Society of Wisconsin, September 17, 1983

The first cases of what is now identified as acquired immune deficiency syndrome (AIDS) were reported two years ago. More than 2,000 cases have been reported nationwide, with perhaps as many as 20 confirmed or suspected cases thus far in Wisconsin. The death rate among AIDS cases is very high.

The cause of AIDS is as yet unknown, as is effective treatment. However, the clinical characteristics of the syndrome have been quite well defined, the scientific and clinical studies are growing rapidly, and to some extent the growing body of knowledge is easing some of the disturbing and seldom documented stories of lack of care available to patients who have or suspect they have AIDS.

The Board of Directors of the State Medical Society considers it important at this stage of the understanding about AIDS to make these observations:

• An open nonjudgmental attitude is basic to all good patient care. The sick individual (heterosexual or homosexual) deserves the best care the profession has to offer for all physical or mental conditions.

• There may be clinical situations which for multiple reasons a physician may not choose to treat. When or if such a situation develops, the ethical course is to refer the patient to another physician.

• Both primary and referral physicians should continue to expand their understanding of this syndrome and provide specific advice on how to prevent personal or blood transmission, especially to persons in those groups which show increased incidence of AIDS.

• The individual physicians and their medical societies, including the State Medical Society, should seek to keep the AIDS problem in perspective through continuing responsible education of the profession and the public, thus reducing the chance of misinterpretation of facts and illfounded deprecation of persons or groups.

The State Medical Society compliments the Section of Acute and Communicable Disease Epidemiology of the Wisconsin Division of Health for its prompt and continuing efforts to update the profession on AIDS. Similarly, the leadership of groups involving homosexually active persons in Wisconsin appear to be acting in a commendably responsible manner to bring about greater understanding of a serious health problem.

Most physicians are aware that the *Journal of the American Medical Association*, the *New England Journal of Medicine*, and Centers for Disease Control publications are highly respected and well read sources for the latest information on AIDS.

Nevertheless, the Society, in support of its expression of policy, will continue to utilize its official publication, the *Wisconsin Medical Journal*, and membership bulletins to provide:

a. widespread dissemination of this statement;

b. updates from the Epidemiology Section of the Division of Health;

c. references to or articles on advice concerning diagnosis, use of lab services, physician referral resources in Wisconsin, information to advise AIDS-susceptible patients, and so on;

d. general information on sexually transmitted diseases and information on how to adequately conduct a sexual activity examination as part of the history and physical;

e. information on medical records and confidentiality;

f. statements by the Wisconsin blood suppliers and processors.

In addition it will encourage professional-sponsored telephone answering services to include in their specialty referral lists physicians or medical centers which have been identified as AIDS referral resources.

At the same time it will encourage all appropriate continuing medical education groups in Wisconsin to give attention not only to the latest scientific and epidemiological updates on AIDS but to the ethical and public educational aspects as well. ∎

PRECAUTIONS ASKED IN DISPOSING BODIES OF AIDS SUSPECT CASES. See NEWS YOU CAN USE, page 68, of the September 1983 issue of the *Wisconsin Medical Journal.*

CALL TOLL-FREE NUMBER FOR INFO ON AIDS. The US Department of Health and Human Services has established a toll-free line to provide the latest medical information on Acquired Immune Deficiency Syndrome (AIDS). The line is open weekdays from 7:30 am to 4:30 pm. The toll-free number is: 1-800-342-AIDS.

25

WISCONSIN MEDICAL JOURNAL, NOVEMBER 1983: VOL. 82

COURTESY OF DICK WAGNER

- There may be clinical situations which for multiple reasons a physician may not choose to treat. When or if such a situation develops, the ethical course is to refer the patient to another physician.

- Both primary and referral physicians should continue to expand their understanding of this syndrome and provide specific advice on how to prevent personal or blood transmission, especially to persons in those groups which show increased incidence of AIDS.

- The individual physicians and their medical societies, including the State Medical Society, should seek to keep the AIDS problem in perspective through continuing responsible education of the profession and the public, thus reducing the chance of misinterpretation of facts and ill-founded deprecation of persons or groups.

Get Active

As the examples in this chapter have shown, there are many ways to get active in the LGBTQ+ movement. By participating in politics, you can really make a difference. Local elections usually have the lowest voter turnout, but local offices have a profound impact on the lives of everyday citizens. We hope this book motivates you to get out, get involved, and get active, because change is always possible.

Conclusion

The LGBTQ+ people, allies, and activists you've read about in this book changed the world by educating themselves, by telling their own stories, by being true to themselves, by building communities, and by getting active. These people made their own contributions to a larger movement. Over the decades, their efforts added up to significant changes in the state and beyond. Today, same-sex marriage is legal in Wisconsin and around the United States. Legal protections in housing, jobs, restaurants, and businesses for LGBTQ+ people are much more common than they were fifty years ago. In fact, attitudes about gay rights have changed faster than attitudes about almost any other social issue in the history of the United States.[1]

In Wisconsin, federal judge Barbara Crabb granted Wisconsin same-sex couples the right to marry on June 6, 2014.[2] In many ways, the fight for LGBTQ+ rights up to that point had centered around the right to marry. Marriage is important because it gives  same-sex couples access to important government recognition and benefits that were previously denied them. It also transformed the community by allowing people to have their love recognized by American society. On June 6, 2014, the Dane County Clerk's office had granted sixty marriage licenses to same-sex couples by noon.[3]

A couple displays signs in support of same-sex marriage at the Marriage Equality Rally in front of the US Supreme Court in Washington, DC, on April 28, 2015, about two months before the *Obergefell v. Hodges* ruling. PHOTO BY ELVERT BARNES

Hundreds of people came to the county courthouse to stand as witnesses to couples who wanted to get married that day.[4]

It was an exciting day for the LGBTQ+ community in Wisconsin. However, at that time, same-sex marriage was still legal only on a state-by-state basis, and Wisconsin was just the twenty-first state to grant that right to same-sex couples. This meant that couples could be considered married in Wisconsin but not in, say, South Dakota. This reality restricted travel and life plans for the couples and their families. As we have seen throughout this book, Wisconsin was again on the forefront of LGBTQ+ rights, but more than half of the United States had yet to catch up.

The following year, 2015, changed that. In the groundbreaking Supreme Court case *Obergefell v. Hodges*, the court voted 5 to 4 to legalize same-sex marriage nationwide. Justice Anthony Kennedy authored the majority opinion, along with Justices Stephen Breyer, Ruth Bader Ginsburg, Elena Kagan, and Sonia Sotomayor.

On June 26, 2015—almost exactly forty-six years after the Stonewall uprising of June 28, 1969—the Supreme Court granted people of all sexual orientations "equal dignity in the eyes of the law":

> No union is more profound than marriage, for it embodies the highest ideals of love, fidelity, devotion, sacrifice, and family. In forming a marital union, two people become something greater than once they were. As some of the petitioners in these cases demonstrate, marriage embodies a love that may endure even past death. It would misunderstand these men and women to say they disrespect the idea of marriage. Their plea is that they do respect it, respect it so deeply that they seek to find its fulfillment for themselves. Their hope is not to be condemned to live in loneliness, excluded from one of civilization's oldest institutions. They ask for equal dignity in the eyes of the law. The Constitution grants them that right. The judgment of the Court of Appeals for the Sixth Circuit is reversed. *It is so ordered.*[5]

Same-sex couples had been allowed to marry in Wisconsin since June 2014, but federal recognition meant that couples would be considered legally married no matter which state they lived in or visited. Many same-sex couples have married since then (including one of this book's authors and her wife), and the above paragraph from Justice Kennedy has become a common reading at those wedding ceremonies. It signifies the US government's recognition of their love and humanity—an incredible change brought about after centuries of criminal treatment.

Yet, LGBTQ+ people still do not receive full protection under the law in America. Here in Wisconsin, as we write this book in 2020, same-sex parents who want to adopt children can still be turned down by adoption agencies because of their gender or sexual orientation. Transgender people can be denied bank loans or credit cards because of their gender identity. Queer and trans

Before same-sex marriage was legal, some couples had union ceremonies. On July 22, 1995, Ken Scott (left) and Brian Bigler (right) were among the first couples in Madison to form a union. Brian worked at Pendarvis (see page 57 for more information on Pendarvis) preserving LGBTQ+ history. WHI IMAGE ID 93363

people of color are still the most vulnerable to discrimination and violence in Wisconsin. Certain Wisconsin counties and cities have passed nondiscrimination ordinances to protect LGBTQ+ people in other ways. Some have banned conversion therapy; others punish crimes committed on the basis of sexual orientation or gender identity. Still, there are no blanket legal protections for LGBTQ+ people nationally or statewide.[6] And we should not forget that the Supreme Court's decision on same-sex marriage passed by a single vote. Marriage equality is the law of the land, for now. But we cannot take for granted that it will be so forever.

While this book was being written in 2020, the Supreme Court of the United States once again took action to provide protections for LGBTQ+ people. In *Bostock v. Clayton County*, the majority of the justices ruled that gay, lesbian, bisexual, transgender, and queer people cannot be disciplined or fired for their sexual orientation or gender identity. Getting active in the court system works and is still working.[7]

This is where your activism comes in. The LGBTQ+ community needs your voice, whether that voice is quiet or loud, written or shouted, full of questions or full of answers. What have you learned from this book about the history of LGBTQ+ activism in Wisconsin? What about these stories surprised you or saddened you or inspired you? How can you continue to work toward realizing the changes these activists hoped to see in our state and country?

All of the people featured in this book were passionate about LGBTQ+ rights. But, just as importantly, they all *persevered*. They kept going, despite obstacles and setbacks, and continued to fight for equality for days and weeks and years.

- Donna Burkett and Manonia Evans were not granted a marriage license when they applied for one in Milwaukee in 1971. Forty-three years later, Wisconsin same-sex couples were asked by county clerks, "Do you want the license to read *bride and bride, groom and groom,* or *spouse and spouse?*"

- Glenway Wescott felt he had to leave Wisconsin and move to the East Coast to live a full, authentic life as a gay man. The state that he found so slow to change in 1928 became the first in the nation to enact a law banning discrimination against homosexuals in 1982.

- Judy Greenspan, an out lesbian, lost the Madison School Board election in 1972. In 1994, Representative Steve Gunderson came out as gay, followed by the election of two other out gay representatives: Tammy Baldwin in 1999 and Mark Pocan in 2012. Wisconsin was the first state in the country to have had three out gay members of Congress. New York State followed in 2020 when its citizens elected the state's second and third out gay Congress members.

None of these changes happened quickly. In some cases, change did not even occur within the initial activists' lifetimes. The changes we work for sometimes come about in ways we can't foresee and on timelines much longer than we would prefer. And occasionally, progress is made and then lost. The important thing is that changes do occur, and those changes matter.

The LGBTQ+ victories of the last half-century are the result of many people educating themselves, telling their stories, being true to themselves, building communities, and actively working for change. They made the lives we lead today possible. It is because of them, and because of you, that we will always be here.

This t-shirt was worn by Bonita S. "Bonnie" Augusta of Madison, who participated in the March on Washington for Lesbian, Gay and Bi Equal Rights and Liberation held on April 25, 1993 (see page 68 for more information on this march). The shirt is now held in the Wisconsin Historical Society's museum collections. We hope it reminds you that, like Bonnie, you are a historymaker! Your actions, words, and belongings tell stories. What will you do, make, or save that will be remembered in the future? How will you change the course of history?
WISCONSIN HISTORICAL SOCIETY MUSEUM #2019.21.1

Appendix A: Map

1. **Eau Claire**
   > The Fire Ball (page 88)
2. **La Crosse**
   > Gay Travel Guides (page 85)
   > *Leaping La Crosse News* (page 47)
3. **Ladysmith**
   > Barry Lynn (page 6)
4. **Ashland**
   > Jamie Nabozny (page 96)
5. **Norwalk**
   > Wisconsin Womyn's Land Cooperative (page 82)
6. **Mineral Point**
   > Bob Neal and Edgar Hellum (page 57)
7. **Hurley**
   > Gay Travel Guides (page 85)
8. **Nekoosa**
   > Selena Meza (page 49)
9. **Oxford**
   > Donna Coleman (page 64)
10. **Madison**
    > Bi?Shy?Why? (page 67)
    > Judy Greenspan (page 99)
    > Lorraine Hansberry (page 3)
    > Lysistrata (page 78)
    > Ron McCrea (page 61)
    > *Our Lives* (page 26)
    > Ted Pierce (page 76)
    > R. Richard Wagner (page 42)
    > Wisconsin State Medical Society (page 107)

11. **Eagle River**
    > Robert Peters (page 9)
12. **Oshkosh**
    > Lloyd Barbee (page 104)
13. **Neenah**
    > Eugene Schrang (page 70)
14. **East Troy**
    > Lorena Hickok (page 10)
15. **Kewaskum**
    > Glenway Wescott (page 39)
16. **Green Bay**
    > Gay Travel Guides (page 85)
17. **Wauwatosa**
    > Lou Sullivan (page 36)
18. **Milwaukee**
    > Donna Burkett and Manonia Evans (page 30)
    > *GPU News* (page 23)
    > Jennifer Hanrahan (page 91)
    > Ralph Kerwineo (page 54)
    > The Queer Zine Archive Project (page 31)
19. **Sheboygan**
    > Adrian Ames (page 21)

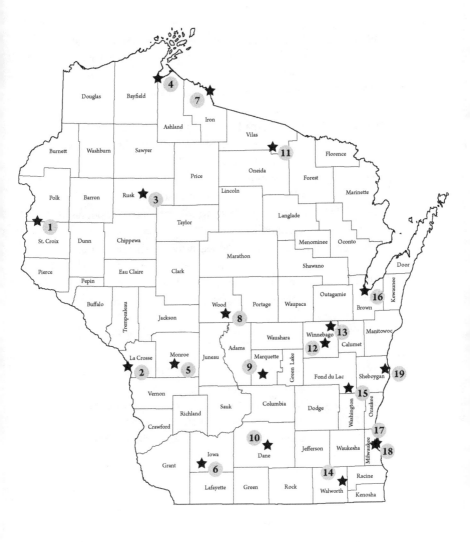

Appendix B: Timeline

1914	Ralph Kerwineo is arrested in Milwaukee for cross-dressing
1928	Glenway Wescott publishes *Good-Bye, Wisconsin* based on his early life in Kewaskum
1934	Bob Neal and Edgar Hellum begin their relationship in Mineral Point
1940s–1950s	Ted Pierce hosts gatherings of gay men in Madison
1950s–1960s	Adrian Ames performs in Sheboygan and other Wisconsin cities as a "female impersonator"
Mid-1960s	Gay travel guides begin to be published around the country highlighting gay-friendly bars in Wisconsin
1966–1970	In Milwaukee, Lou Sullivan writes diary entries about his gender identity
1967	Representative Lloyd Barbee introduces the first bill that would decriminalize homosexuality in Wisconsin
1969	The Stonewall uprising occurs in New York City
1970s	Donna Coleman cofounds the Forker Motorcycle Club in Milwaukee
1971	Milwaukee's Gay People's Union publishes its first issue of *GPU News*
1971	Donna Burkett and Manonia Evans file suit to obtain a marriage license in Milwaukee
1973	Judy Greenspan runs for the Madison School Board
1977	Lysistrata opens a restaurant and lounge in Madison
1977	The Wisconsin Womyn's Land Cooperative in Norwalk is founded
1978	*Leaping La Crosse News* publishes its first issue
1982	Ron McCrea is announced as Governor Tony Earl's press chief
1983	The State Medical Society of Wisconsin publishes its "Statement Concerning AIDS"
1987	Out elected officials from Dane County attend the Second National March on Washington for Lesbian and Gay Rights

1990s–2000s	Dr. Eugene Schrang performs gender confirmation surgeries in Neenah
1992	Bi?Shy?Why? is founded in Madison
1994	Jennifer Hanrahan's essay about being bisexual in Milwaukee is published in *Two Teenagers in Twenty*
1996	Jamie Nabozny wins his court case against the Ashland School District
2003	The Queer Zine Archive Project is established in Milwaukee
2009	*Our Lives* is founded in Madison
2011	The Fire Ball drag show is founded in Eau Claire
2014	Same-sex couples are granted the right to marry in Wisconsin
2015	The Supreme Court legalizes same-sex marriage nationwide
2017	Selena Meza records their oral history about growing up in Nekoosa
2019–2020	R. Richard Wagner publishes two books on Wisconsin's gay history

Appendix C:
Additional Resources

Online Resources

- Comprehensive list of LGBTQ terms and definitions: www.its
  pronouncedmetrosexual.com/2013/01/a-comprehensive-list
  -of-lgbtq-term-definitions/
- GLAAD glossary of LGBTQ terms: www.glaad.org/reference/
  lgbtq
- GLSEN (Gay, Lesbian, Straight Education Network): www
  .glsen.org/
- GSAFE (Gay Straight Alliance for Safe Schools): https://
  gsafewi.org/
- Human Rights Campaign: www.hrc.org/
- Human Rights Campaign Glossary of Terms: www.hrc.org/
  resources/glossary-of-terms
- LGBTQ+ Archive at UW–Milwaukee Libraries: https://guides
  .library.uwm.edu/archives-lgbt
- Madison's LGBTQ Community at the UW–Madison Archives:
  www.library.wisc.edu/archives/exhibits/madisons-lgbt-community
  -1960s-to-present/
- Personal Pronouns: www.mypronouns.org/
- Queer People of Color Resource Guide: https://lgbt.wisc.edu/
  documents/qpoc-crossroads-resource-guide/
- Two-Spirit Resource Guide: https://lgbt.wisc.edu/documents/
  two-spirit-resource-directory/

- UW–Madison Gender and Sexuality Campus Center: https://lgbt.wisc.edu/
- Wisconsin LGBT History Project: www.mkelgbthist.org/
- Wisconsin LGBTQ Summit: www.wilgbtqsummit.org/

Book Resources

- Boughner, Terry. *Out of All Time: A Gay and Lesbian History.* Boston: Alyson Publications, 1988.
- Bronski, Michael and Richie Chevat. *A Queer History of the United States for Young People.* Boston: Beacon Press, 2019.
- Carter, David. *Stonewall: The Riots That Sparked The Gay Revolution.* New York: St. Martin's Press, 2004.
- Cenziper, Debbie, and James Obergefell. *Love Wins: The Promise That Won the Landmark Case for Marriage Equality.* South Melbourne, Victoria: Affirm Press, 2016.
- Faderman, Lillian. *The Gay Revolution: The Story of the Struggle.* New York: Simon & Schuster, 2016.
- Feinberg, Leslie. *Transgender Warriors: Making History from Joan of Arc to Dennis Rodman.* Boston: Beacon Press, 2005.
- Fellows, Will. *Farm Boys: Lives of Gay Men from the Rural Midwest.* Madison: University of Wisconsin Press, 1996.
- Mumford, Kevin J. *Not Straight, Not White: Black Gay Men from the March on Washington to the AIDS Crisis.* Chapel Hill: University of North Carolina Press, 2016.
- Sebenthall, Betty (aka Roberta Hill). *The Desperate Wall.* New York: G.P. Putnam's Sons, 1949.
- Segal, Mark. *And Then I Danced: Traveling the Road to LGBT Equality.* New York, Akashic Books, 2015.
- Wagner, R. Richard. *Coming Out, Moving Forward: Wisconsin's Recent Gay History.* Madison: Wisconsin Historical Society Press, 2020.

- Wagner, R. Richard. *We Have Always Been Here: Wisconsin's Early Gay History*. Madison: Wisconsin Historical Society Press, 2019.
- Wescott, Glenway. *Good-Bye, Wisconsin*. New York: Harper & Bros., 1928.

Resources by Chapter

Introduction

- Ho-Chunk Two-Spirit: https://ourlivesmadison.com/article/a-tale-of-two-spirits/
- Gay Liberation Front: http://web-static.nypl.org/exhibitions/1969/liberation.html

Chapter 1

- *The Ladder* at the University of California–Berkeley Library: https://digitalassets.lib.berkeley.edu/sfbagals/The_Ladder/tl_index.html
- Gay People's Union Collection at UW–Milwaukee: https://uwdc.library.wisc.edu/collections/gpu/
- Queer Zine Archive Project: www.qzap.org
- *Our Lives* Magazine: https://ourliveswisconsin.com/

Chapter 2

- *Leaping La Crosse News* collection at UW–La Crosse's Murphy Library Digital Collections: https://recollectionwisconsin.org/collections/leaping-la-crosse-news
- Glenway Wescott: www.mkelgbthist.org/people/peo-w/wescott_glenway.htm
- Digital Transgender Archive: www.digitaltransgenderarchive.net/
- Lou Sullivan: www.wuwm.com/post/turning-challenges-fuel-story-trans-activist-lou-sullivan#stream/0; Louis Sullivan,

From Female to Male: The Life of Jack Bee Garland (Boston: Alyson Publications, 1990).

Chapter 3

- Ralph Kerwineo: Matthew J. Prigge, "The 'Girl-Man' of Milwaukee: The Lives of Cora Anderson," *Wisconsin Magazine of History* 96, No. 3 (Spring 2013): 14–27.
- Pendarvis: https://pendarvis.wisconsinhistory.org/
- *Bi-Lines* collection at the UW–Madison Archives: https://search.library.wisc.edu/catalog/999712915802121
- Ronald A. "Ron" McCrea Papers at the Wisconsin Historical Society Archives: https://search.library.wisc.edu/catalog/9911125048402121
- Lesbian Lizards: https://ourlivesmadison.com/article/lizard-legacy/

Chapter 4

- Theodore "Ted" Pierce papers at the Wisconsin Historical Society Archives: https://search.library.wisc.edu/catalog/999464284302121
- OutReach: www.outreachmadisonlgbt.org/
- Ann Heron, ed., *Two Teenagers in Twenty: Writings by Gay and Lesbian Youth* (Boston: Alyson Publications, 1994).
- Lysistrata: http://lostwomynsspace.blogspot.com/2011/10/lysistrata-restaurant.html

Chapter 5

- Jamie Nabozny court case: www.lambdalegal.org/in-court/cases/nabozny-v-podlesny
- Judy Greenspan papers at the UW–Madison Archives: https://search.library.wisc.edu/catalog/9912201445702121; Judy Greenspan, "Memoirs of a Tired Lesbian," *Whole Woman* (October 1972).

- Kathleen Nichols/Barbara Constans papers at the Wisconsin Historical Society Archives: https://search.library.wisc.edu/catalog/9911124450802121; "Know Your Madisonian: Kathleen Nichols," *Wisconsin State Journal*, April 6, 2006.
- Daphne E. Barbee-Wooten, ed., *Justice for All: Selected Writings of Lloyd A. Barbee* (Madison: Wisconsin Historical Society Press, 2017).
- Norman Richards, ed., *Heart Pieces: Wisconsin Poets for AIDS* (Milwaukee: Namron Press, 1987).
- HIV/AIDS: www.hiv.gov/hiv-basics/overview/about-hiv-and-aids/what-are-hiv-and-aids; www.dhs.wisconsin.gov/publications/p02441.pdf

Conclusion

- *Obergefell v. Hodges* gay marriage case: www.supremecourt.gov/opinions/14pdf/14-556_3204.pdf
- *Bostock v. Clayton* LGBT employment discrimination case: www.supremecourt.gov/opinions/19pdf/17-1618_hfci.pdf

Acknowledgments

First, we want to thank the teens, who are our inspiration and our future. Special thanks goes to those teens who completed surveys about the sources in this book and provided feedback during the height of the COVID-19 pandemic. Their words can be found throughout the book and their names are Braiya, Charlotte, Cora, Eva, Evan, Ginger, Isabelle, and Theresa.

Thank you to Brian Juchems at GSAFE for sharing our survey (and planning to let us present before the coronavirus changed the world). Thank you to Joan Jacobson, for your dedication as an educator and for talking with us about your decades of work and experience leading LGBTQ+ education efforts in a Wisconsin high school.

Thank you to Dick Wagner! Your kindness and assistance was invaluable. The foundational work you have done as the historian of Wisconsin's LGBTQ+ movement, and also as a government official and activist, is inspirational.

Thank you to Kate Thompson, Liz Wyckoff, and the Wisconsin Historical Society Press staff for all of your guidance. This book is what it is because of your efforts, and particularly because of Liz's dedication and patience. Thank you for spinning our ideas into gold.

Lastly, this project would not exist without the brave and amazing people who appear in the pages of this book. Their work changed the world. And, thank you to the donors to this project, many of whom are the very historymakers whose voices we are seeking to amplify in this work. It is because of you that today's teens will continue to grow Wisconsin's legacy.

• • • • • • • • • • • • •

Thank you to the Wisconsin Historical Society for undertaking important projects like this, and specific thanks to Alicia Goehring and Kate Thompson, who believed in me enough to entrust me with the authorship of this amazing project. Bethany Brander and Susan Caya-Slusser at Pendarvis were also a great help in sharing their recent work.

Throughout the process of writing this book I reflected on my own teen years and the people who first inspired me to become an ally—especially Allen Kienbaum, who is the Reginald to my Margaret, and Clint Drake, a fellow Fellow and amazing friend who asked for an autographed copy but deserves so much more.

Thank you to Kathy and Len Kalvaitis, and to Katie, Ron, Leo, and Kat, whose love and support is unending. May Kat and Leo grow up and live in a more accepting and better world. Special thanks to my mom who is the first editor of everything I write. In my journey, so many friends and family members taught me the importance of love and life. I carry their wisdom in my heart and mind. I also appreciate the moral support and frequent book inquiries Anna Lange made during our long, solitary months of quarantine. Our conversations helped immensely! I often say I would not be where I am today without Dr. Rebecca K. Shrum, who helped me see how using history to change the world could be a profession and not just a personal pursuit.

Very importantly, thank you to the amazing Kristen Whitson, who jumped into this project the minute I asked. While our timeline was grueling, there is no one I would rather write with. To the best co-author ever—my Tuesday nights will never be the same.

—Jenny Kalvaitis

Thank you to my wife, Gaia, who believes in the things I'm capable of long before I do. I love you beyond words. Being married to you gives me strength and inspiration to fight for this kind of life for everyone.

And to S & S: thank you for letting me into your hearts as a bonus mom, and for letting me know you and learn from you. I wanted to write this book because I wish it had been in your lives earlier. You are brave and powerful humans who will change the world in ways big and small.

To Jodie Jens, elementary school guidance counselor, and Judy Reynolds, sixth grade teacher. They told me when I was ten years old that I would write a book. I didn't believe them. They were so sure they said I had to dedicate my first book to them; their confidence shaped the person I became. May all kids have adults who believe in them so fervently.

My whole family, both born and married: this book belongs to you too. Mom; Gretchen and Dan; Dave and Terri: may every gay kid have parents as unconditionally supportive as you are.

To Dano, the ultimate ally. Always.

Thank you to KJD, whose appearance in my life started me on the path to working in archives and without whom I would not have learned a thing about LGBTQ+ archives. Likewise, a huge thanks to the Madison LGBTQ+ Archives folks for their enthusiasm, support, and unquestioning acceptance of a budding archivist: Scott Seyforth, Michele Besant, Dick Wagner, Katherine Charek Briggs, Kalleen Mortenson, Pat Calchina, and especially Katie Nash, Troy Reeves, and Cat Phan. Thank you for not saying a thing when you found me crying over artifacts again.

The UW–Madison Information School provided me with a stellar education and lots of support and intellectual space to roam through these topics. Thanks go to Michele Besant again, Ethelene

Whitmire, Dorothea Salo, Vicki Tobias, and Michael Edmonds. Omar Poler and George Greendeer opened up a world of Indigenous archiving for me that is represented in the First Nations people in this book. My classmates and soul-friends Joey, Monica, and Bailey listened to me toss around ideas and pushed for greater representation; their contributions are all over these pages.

To Stephanie, who brings glitter and laughter and hugs and high heels to every occasion. You've taught me so much about authenticity, determination, fierce mothering, and friendship.

I have been the fortunate recipient of a fantastic education my whole life, and teachers who believed in me kept me moving year by year. They heard my passion for justice and supported me in navigating the world to enact it. Vic Passante, especially, taught me to use my resourcefulness to change the world.

Finally, and most importantly, to my co-author Jenny Kalvaitis: working on this project with you has been such a joy. Thank you for asking me to join you in creating this essential resource, and for all the support and encouragement as we wrote our hearts out. It's an honor to see my name alongside yours on this book.

—Kristen Whitson

Notes

Introduction

1. R. Richard Wagner, *We've Been Here All Along: Wisconsin's Early Gay History* (Madison: Wisconsin Historical Society Press, 2019), 178–182.
2. Susan Quinn, *Eleanor and Hick: The Love Affair That Shaped a First Lady* (New York: Penguin Books, 2017).
3. "Primary Source Analysis Tool | Teachers—Library of Congress," Primary Source Analysis Tool, Library of Congress, www.loc.gov/teachers/primary -source-analysis-tool/.
4. Nikki Mandell and Bobbie Malone, *Thinking Like a Historian: Rethinking History Instruction: A Framework to Enhance and Improve Teaching and Learning* (Madison: Wisconsin Historical Society Press, 2007).
5. Merriam-Webster.com Dictionary, s.v. "deadname," August 18, 2020, www .merriam-webster.com/dictionary/deadname.
6. Wagner, *We've Been Here All Along*.
7. Nancy Oestreich Lurie, "Winnebago Berdache," *American Anthropologist* 55, no. 5 (December 1953): 708–712, https://doi.org/10.1525/aa.1953.55.5.02a 00090.
8. Susan Ferentinos, *Interpreting LGBT History at Museums and Historic Sites* (Lanham: Rowman & Littlefield, 2015), 30.
9. Elizabeth Reis, "Impossible Hermaphrodites: Intersex in America, 1620–1960," *Journal of American History* 92, no. 2 (September 1, 2005): 411–441, https://doi .org/10.2307/3659273.
10. I. Bennett Capers, "Cross Dressing and the Criminal," *Yale Journal of Law and the Humanities* 9 (2008), https://pdfs.semanticscholar.org/eeb9/fbbe5230cee13 162de97a94f7217e45ff812.pdf.
11. Wagner, *We've Been Here All Along*, 254.
12. Wagner, *We've Been Here All Along*, 278–280.
13. Jill Davey, NLFO Newsletter, January 1, 1981, *Leaping La Crosse News* collection, Murphy Library Digital Collections, UW–La Crosse, La Crosse, WI, https://digitalcollections.uwlax.edu/jsp/RcWebImageViewer.jsp?doc _id=d3bacbc6-b596-448c-9431-3391dfe846d1/wlacu000/00000022/00000008.
14. Ferentinos, *Interpreting LGBT History at Museums and Historic Sites*, 81.

15. Dale Hillerman, "Gay Counseling Program History," LGBT Collection, UW–Madison Archives, 2015/304, 10.

16. R. Richard Wagner, *Coming Out, Moving Forward: Wisconsin's Recent Gay History* (Madison: Wisconsin Historical Society Press, 2020).

Chapter 1

1. R. Richard Wagner, *We've Been Here All Along: Wisconsin's Early Gay History* (Madison: Wisconsin Historical Society Press, 2019), 7–18.

2. Wisconsin LGBTQ History Project, "Milwaukee's love affair with drag isn't a new phenomenon." Facebook, August 11, 2019, www.facebook.com/pg/wislgbtq history/posts/.

3. R. Richard Wagner, *Coming Out, Moving Forward: Wisconsin's Recent Gay History* (Madison: Wisconsin Historical Society Press, 2020), 21.

4. "Eldon Murray—People in the History of Gay and Lesbian Life in Milwaukee, Wisconsin," Wisconsin LGBTQ History Project, September 2020, www.mkelgb thist.org/people/peo-m/murray_eldon.htm.

5. Wagner, *Coming Out, Moving Forward*, 20.

6. "Our Lives Magazine—Print Media in the History of Gay and Lesbian Life in Milwaukee, Wisconsin," Wisconsin LGBT History Project, July 2020, www .mkelgbthist.org/media/print/our-lives.htm.

7. "The Ladder | ONE Archives," ONE Archives at the USC Libraries, https://one .usc.edu/archive-location/ladder.

8. Daughters of Bilitis, "Cross Currents," *The Ladder*, 1972, https://digitalassets.lib .berkeley.edu/sfbagals/The_Ladder/1972_Ladder_Vol16_No05-06_Feb_Mar.pdf.

9. "About the Archive," QZAP—Queer Zine Archive, 2014, https://archive.qzap.org/ index.php/About/Index.

10. Lainey Seyler, "The Largest Independent LGBTQ Zine Collection Is Stored in a Riverwest Basement, and You Can See Some of It Online," *Milwaukee Journal Sentinel*, July 9, 2018, www.jsonline.com/story/entertainment/2018/07/09/there -2-500-queer-punk-zines-riverwest-basement/755636002/.

11. Seyler, "The Largest Independent LGBTQ Zine Collection."

Chapter 2

1. Eldon Murray, "I Remember Lou Sullivan," ed. Susan Stryker, *FTM Newsletter*, Summer 2007, 1; Lou Sullivan, "Lou Sullivan in His Own Words," ed. Susan Stryker, *FTM Newsletter*, Summer 2007, 3.

2. Lou Sullivan, *Information for the Female-To-Male Crossdresser and Transsexual*, 2nd ed. (San Francisco, 1985), www.digitaltransgenderarchive.net/downloads/ g158bh442.

3. Jerry Roscoe, *Glenway Wescott Personally: A Biography* (Madison: University of Wisconsin Press, 2002).

4. R. Richard Wagner, *We've Been Here All Along: Wisconsin's Early Gay History* (Madison: Wisconsin Historical Society Press, 2019), 84.

5. R. Richard Wagner, email message to authors, May 22, 2020.

6. R. Richard Wagner and Lisa Speckhard, "Q&A: Longtime Madison Activist Dick Wagner Writes Book on Gay History of Wisconsin," *Capital Times* (Madison, WI), November 20, 2016, https://madison.com/ct/news/local/govt-and-politics/q-a-longtime-madison-activist-dick-wagner-writes-book-on/article_d2ff83fe-b783-54de-a728-ac6b81041c6a.html.

7. "Oral History: Defined," Oral History Association, www.oralhistory.org/about/do-oral-history/.

Chapter 3

1. "Girl-Man Now Is Free Again," *Milwaukee Journal*, May 7, 1914; "Girl Lives as Man and Weds," *Milwaukee Journal*, May 3, 1914.

2. "Girl Carried Out Part as Man with Great Skill," *Milwaukee Journal*, May 5, 1914.

3. Matthew J. Prigge, "The 'Girl-Man' of Milwaukee: The Lives of Cora Anderson," *Wisconsin Magazine of History* 96, No. 3 (Spring 2013): 14–27, https://content.wisconsinhistory.org/digital/collection/wmh/id/51538/rec/3.

4. "Man-Girl Hypnotized Asserts Father at Kendallville, Ind.," *Milwaukee Journal*, May 5, 1914.

5. "Girl-Man Is Free" *Milwaukee Sentinel Evening*, May 7, 1914.

6. Bethany Brander, "All Roads Lead to Pendarvis House: Celebrating a Preservation and Culinary Legacy," *Wisconsin Magazine of History* 104, No. 1 (Fall 2020): 28–39.

7. Scott Seyforth and Dick Wagner, "Ron McCrea Collection," Madison LGBTQ Archive, December 20, 2019, https://madisonlgbtq.tumblr.com/search/McCrea.

8. "GLAAD Media Reference Guide–Lesbian/Gay/Bisexual Glossary of Terms," GLAAD, accessed July 31, 2020, https://glaad.org/reference/lgbtq.

9. R. Richard Wagner, *Coming Out, Moving Forward: Wisconsin's Recent Gay History* (Madison: Wisconsin Historical Society Press, 2020), 285–287, 312–314.

10. "Obituary: Ronald Alan 'Ron' McCrea," *Channel 3000*, January 25, 2020, www.channel3000.com/ronald-alan-ron-mccrea/.

11. Wagner, *Coming Out, Moving Forward*, 107–108.

12. Nadine Smith, "The 20th Anniversary of the LGBT March on Washington: How Far Have We Come?," *Huffington Post*, February 2, 2016, www.huffpost.com/entry/the-20th-anniversary-of-the-lgbt-march-on-washington_b_3149185.

13. Amin Ghaziani, *The Dividends of Dissent: How Conflict and Culture Work in Lesbian and Gay Marches on Washington* (Chicago: University of Chicago Press, 2008), 151.

14. Wagner, *Coming Out, Moving Forward*, 106.

15. Wagner, *Coming Out, Moving Forward*, 106.

16. "Plastic Surgeon Performs over 100 Sex Changes a Year," *Journal Times* (Racine County, WI), August 15, 1995, https://journaltimes.com/news/national/plastic-surgeon-performs-over-sex-changes-a-year/article_3ba43f26-50e1-529d-8dad-032ee474c2b8.html.

17. "What Is Gender Dysphoria?" American Psychiatric Association, February 2016, www.psychiatry.org/patients-families/gender-dysphoria/what-is-gender-dysphoria.

18. Pamela De Groff, "Left of Center," Tennessee Vals Newsletter, August 2001, www.tvals.org/oldsite/Newsletters/VNL2001Aug.html.

19. Andrea James, "Eugene Schrang Archive," Transgender Map, October 8, 2019, www.transgendermap.com/medical/surgery/usa/wisconsin/eugene-schrang/.

Chapter 4

1. R. Richard Wagner, *We've Been Here All Along: Wisconsin's Early Gay History* (Madison: Wisconsin Historical Society Press, 2019), 118–169.

2. "To the Committee of the MARQUETTE*WILLIAMSON Garden Tour," Ted Pierce Papers, box 2, folder 5, Wisconsin Historical Society Archives, Madison, WI.

3. Wagner, *We've Been Here All Along*, 302–306.

4. Wagner, *We've Been Here All Along*, 142–143.

5. International Co-operative Alliance, "Cooperative Identity, Values & Principles," www.ica.coop/en/cooperatives/cooperative-identity.

6. Ariel Levy, "Lesbian Nation," *New Yorker*, February 23, 2009, www.newyorker.com/magazine/2009/03/02/lesbian-nation.

7. R. Richard Wagner, "To Enclave or Not to Enclave," *Our Lives Magazine* (September 2016), https://ourlivesmadison.com/article/to-enclave-or-not-to-enclave/.

8. Paul Masterson, "Daughters of the Earth Continues to Offer a Rural Respite for Womyn," *Shepherd Express*, October 15, 2019, https://shepherdexpress.com/lgbtq/my-lgbtq-pov/daughters-of-the-earth-continues-to-offer-a-rural-respite-fo/.

9. Michelle Goldberg, "What Is a Woman?," *New Yorker*, July 28, 2014, www.newyorker.com/magazine/2014/08/04/woman-2.

10. "Chronology of Guides to Wisconsin Gay Venues Prior to Local Periodicals—Print Media in the History of Gay and Lesbian Life in Milwaukee, Wisconsin," Wisconsin LGBT History Project, www.mkelgbthist.org/media/guide-chronology.htm.

11. "Places of Interest: A Guide That Works," page 1, Wisconsin LGBT History Project, www.mkelgbthist.org/media/guides/places/places80-p001.jpg.

12. R. Richard Wagner, *Coming Out, Moving Forward: Wisconsin's Recent Gay History* (Madison: Wisconsin Historical Society Press, 2020), 294.

13. Wagner, *Coming Out, Moving Forward*, 369, 398.

14. Denise Olson, "UW–Eau Claire Ranked No. 3 in Country for LGBTQ-Friendly Colleges," University of Wisconsin–Eau Claire website, May 11, 2017, www.uwec.edu/news/equity-diversity-inclusion/lgbtq-friendly-rankings-2353/.

15. Niko Bell, "One in 10 People Are Gay? Not Even Close," *Xtra Magazine*, December 5, 2014, www.dailyxtra.com/one-in-10-people-are-gay-not-even-close-65341.

16. Diaman, July 16, 2008, book review, "One Teenager in Ten," www.goodreads.com/book/show/1436965.One_Teenager_in_Ten.

Chapter 5

1. US Constitution, Preamble.
2. R. Richard Wagner, *Coming Out, Moving Forward: Wisconsin's Recent Gay History* (Madison: Wisconsin Historical Society Press, 2020), 259.
3. Wagner, *Coming Out, Moving Forward*, 259.
4. "*Nabozny v. Podlesny*," Lambda Legal, www.lambdalegal.org/in-court/cases/nabozny-v-podlesny.
5. "$900,000 Won by Gay Man in Abuse Case," *New York Times*, November 21, 1996, sec. U.S., www.nytimes.com/1996/11/21/us/900000-won-by-gay-man-in-abuse-case.html.
6. Chuck Stewart, *Gay and Lesbian Issues: A Reference Handbook* (Oxford: ABC-CLIO, 2003), 59.
7. Jamie Nabozny, "Jamie Nabozny | Safe School Advocate," www.jamienabozny.com.
8. Wagner, *Coming Out, Moving Forward*, 65–67.
9. Dave Cieslewicz, "A Museum of Our Own," *Isthmus*, July 18, 2019, https://isthmus.com/news/cover-story/does-madison-history-need-its-own-space/.
10. "A Crowded School Board List Starts Sorting Out," *Capital Times*, February 15, 1973.
11. "Vote Greenspan for School Board," *Whole Woman*, February 1973; "School Board Candidate Runs on Gay Platform," *Capital Times*, February 5, 1973.
12. "You Are Here: Finding LGBTQ Community," An Exhibit Guide of the Madison LGBTQ Archive, April 27, 2017, 4, https://issuu.com/madisonlgbtq/docs/booklet; Wagner, *Coming Out, Moving Forward*, 67.
13. Eileen Boyce, "Veteran Activist Returns to Madison," *Badger Herald*, September 11, 2001, https://badgerherald.com/news/2001/09/11/veteran-activist-ret/.
14. Bill Meunier, "Wisconsin Marches on Washington, D.C.," *Wisconsin Light*, November 20, 1987.
15. Meunier, "Wisconsin Marches on Washington, D.C."
16. William Dahlk, "Lloyd Augustus Barbee," Encyclopedia of Milwaukee, 2016, https://emke.uwm.edu/entry/lloyd-augustus-barbee/; Judith Siers-Poisson, "Daughter Recalls Wisconsin's Lloyd Barbee and a Life Spent Fighting for Justice," Wisconsin Public Radio, October 18, 2017, www.wpr.org/daughter-recalls-wisconsins-lloyd-barbee-and-life-spent-fighting-justice.
17. Wagner, *Coming Out, Moving Forward*, 204–207.
18. Daphne E. Barbee-Wooten, ed., *Justice for All: Selected Writings of Lloyd A. Barbee* (Madison, WI: Wisconsin Historical Society Press, 2017).
19. "The History of the Quilt," National AIDS Memorial, www.aidsmemorial.org/quilt-history.
20. "UW Hospital's HIV Clinic Brings AIDS Memorial Quilt to Madison," news.wisc.edu, December 1, 2009, https://news.wisc.edu/uw-hospitals-hiv-clinic-brings-aids-memorial-quilt-to-madison/; Lucky Tomaszek, "AIDS Quilt Panels Coming to MAM," *Wisconsin Gazette*, June 3, 2010, www.mkelgbthist.org/media/print/wis-gazette/issues-v01-05/WiG-v01-15.pdf.

21. Wagner, *Coming Out, Moving Forward*, 321.
22. "HIV/AIDS," *World Health Organization*, August 29, 2018, www.who.int/data/gho/data/themes/hiv-aids.

Conclusion

1. Shankar Vedantam, "Radically Normal: How Gay Rights Activists Changed the Minds of Their Opponents," Hidden Brain, National Public Radio, April 8, 2019, www.npr.org/transcripts/709567750.
2. Jessie Opoien, "District Court Overturns Wisconsin's Gay Marriage Ban," *Capital Times*, June 6, 2014, https://madison.com/ct/news/local/writers/jessie-opoien/district-court-overturns-wisconsin-s-gay-marriage-ban/article_e1258857-731c-569e-b759-11c5aba089bd.html.
3. Jessie Opoien, "Second Day of Legal Same-Sex Marriages in Dane County—'It's Been Amazing,'" *Capital Times*, June 7, 2014, https://madison.com/ct/news/local/writers/jessie-opoien/second-day-of-legal-same-sex-marriages-in-dane-county-its-been-amazing/article_d5e048c4-ee68-11e3-887d-0019bb2963f4.html.
4. Opoien, "Second Day of Legal Same-Sex Marriages in Dane County."
5. *Obergefell et al v. Hodges*, 135 US 28 (2015).
6. "Wisconsin's Equality Profile," Movement Advancement Project, www.lgbtmap.org/equality_maps/profile_state/WI.
7. *Bostock v. Clayton County*, 590 US (2020).

Index

About the Authors

Courtesy of Jenny Kalvaitis

Jenny Kalvaitis has a Master's degree in Public History from Indiana University–Purdue University Indianapolis, and she has worked in informal education and museum education for over ten years.

Photo by Shalicia Johnson

Kristen Whitson has a Master's degree in Library and Information Studies from the University of Wisconsin–Madison, and she has worked in digital preservation, community and indigenous archives, and LGBTQ+ archives.